**Creative Alchemy**

*Revealing the Secret Equation to Creative Excellence*

# OrangeBooks Publication

1st Floor, Rajhans Arcade, Mall Road, Kohka, Bhilai, Chhattisgarh 490020

Website: **www.orangebooks.in**

---

**© Copyright, 2024, Author**

All rights reserved. No part of this book may be reproduced, stored in a retrieval system, or transmitted, in any form by any means, electronic, mechanical, magnetic, optical, chemical, manual, photocopying, recording or otherwise, without the prior written consent of its writer.

**First Edition, 2024**

**ISBN:** 978-93-6554-437-4

# THE CREATIVE ALCHEMY

REVEALING
THE SECRET
EQUATION TO
CREATIVE
EXCELLENCE

**SHIREESH JAIN**

OrangeBooks Publication
www.orangebooks.in

# *Preface: The Path to Creative Excellence*

Every outstanding creation begins with question—a spark of curiosity that ignites a deeper exploration. Whether you are an artist, an entrepreneur, a leader, or simply someone looking to transform ideas into reality, the pursuit of creative excellence is universal. Yet, creative excellence is often misunderstood. People often perceive creative excellence as an elusive gift, reserved for a select few, while creative excellence is a process—one that anyone can cultivate.

This book, The Creative Alchemy, is your guide to understanding and mastering that process. Inspired by timeless stories and real-world examples, it will take you on a journey to uncover the Equation for creative excellence. Through a blend of storytelling, theories, exercises, and actionable insights, you will learn how to transform your raw ideas into something valuable—just like the alchemist who turns base metal into gold.

The book begins with the story of Elias, a curious young man who seeks out the legendary Alchemist, not for the wealth of gold but for the knowledge of how to create it. As you follow Elias's journey, you will discover, alongside him, the five key elements of creative excellence: curiosity, courage, cognition, collaboration, and consistency. Each chapter will explore these elements in depth, providing you with practical exercises and real-life examples to apply to your own creative pursuits.

In Chapter 2, you will be introduced to the Creative Excellence Equation—a structure that integrates these five elements into a cohesive process. The equation begins with curiosity, the spark that drives innovation, and progresses through the courage to take risks, the cognitive tools needed to refine ideas, the power of collaboration, and the importance of consistency in seeing ideas through to completion.

Subsequent chapters delve deeper into each of these components. You will explore how to cultivate curiosity by asking the right questions, how to embrace failure as part of the creative journey, and how to collaborate with others to strengthen your ideas. You will also learn how to overcome the conceptual blocks—those mental weeds such as fear, doubt, and perfectionism—that often hold us back from achieving our full creative potential.

Throughout the book, you will find examples of innovators, leaders, and creators who applied these principles in their own lives—people like Steve Jobs, Elon Musk, and Richard Feynman, who turned their visions into reality. You will also encounter practical exercises that will help you apply the Creative Excellence Equation to your own projects, whether personal or professional.

This book is a toolkit for action, not just a theoretical guide. Each chapter builds upon the last, guiding you deeper into the creative process. By the end, you will have the knowledge and tools to take your ideas from seeds to fruition and refine your raw materials into gold.

Creative excellence is not magic, nor is it reserved for the few. It is a process that, with the right mindset and tools, anyone can master. I invite you to embark on this journey of discovery, to remove the weeds that hold you back, and to cultivate the elements that will lead you to creative excellence.

Welcome to "The Creative Alchemy." Let us begin.

# *Acknowledgments*

The journey of writing The Creative Alchemy has been one of discovery, challenge, and growth, and it would not have been possible without the support and inspiration of many people.

First, I want to express my deepest gratitude to my family. Your unwavering belief in me has always been my greatest source of strength. Thank you for your patience, understanding, and constant encouragement, especially during the long hours spent refining each page.

To my mentors, friends, and colleagues who have fueled my curiosity and guided my thinking—thank you for your wisdom, insights, and conversations that helped shape this work. Your experiences and stories, both personal and professional, have enriched my understanding of creative excellence and its forms.

I would also like to acknowledge the great thinkers, innovators, and creators whose work has inspired me and countless others. The lessons learned from pioneers like Steve Jobs, Richard Feynman, Elon Musk, and others have profoundly influenced the principles within this book. Their boldness, curiosity, and resilience in the face of challenges continue to serve as guiding lights on the path to creative excellence.

A special thanks to the readers who took the time to share their thoughts, feedback, and perspectives on early drafts of this book. Your contributions have been invaluable in refining the final product, and your enthusiasm for the ideas within these pages motivates me to continue sharing what I have learned.

Finally, to all those who are embarking on their own creative journeys: this book is for you. It is my hope that the ideas, tools, and stories shared here will inspire you to unlock your own creative potential and to never stop exploring, questioning, and creating.

Thank you all for being a part of this journey.

# Table of Contents

## Chapter 1
The Alchemist's Secret .......................................................... 1

## Chapter 2
Decoding the Creative Excellence Equation ........................... 14

## Chapter 3
Curiosity—The Spark of Creative Alchemy ......................... 25

## Chapter 4
Courage—The Fuel of Creative Alchemy ............................. 42

## Chapter 5
Cognition—The Crucible of Creative Alchemy ................... 58

## Chapter 6
Collaboration: The Catalyst for Creative Alchemy ............ 74

## Chapter 7
*Consistency—The Oxygen that Sustains the Creative Flame* .................................................. 89

## Chapter 8
*Purging Contaminants — Overcoming Conceptual Blocks* ................................................ 98

## Chapter 9
*Creative excellence in Action: Real-World Case Studies* ........................................................ 111

## Chapter 10
*Conclusion: Mastering the Creative Excellence Equation* ................................................. 131

## References ............................................................ 139

# Chapter 1
# The Alchemist's Secret

Once, upon a time cloaked in legend, there was a man known as the **Great Alchemist**. He lived alone in a secluded workshop deep within a forest, where ancient trees stretched skyward, their tops lost to the mist. His workshop, nestled at the foot of a mountain, seemed to be guarded by nature itself, shielding the secrets within from the curious and the greedy.

The Great Alchemist was a figure shrouded in mystery. His name had faded into obscurity, and his face was rarely seen by the outside world. Those fortunate enough to encounter him spoke of a man draped in flowing robes, with silver hair shimmering like moonlight and eyes that sparkled with wisdom drawn from countless experiences. His hands, weathered from years of experimentation, moved with grace and intent.

For decades, kings, merchants, and scholars sought him out, eager to learn his secrets. They traveled through perilous paths and dense forests, bringing treasures—chests filled with gold, jewels, and spices—offering kingdoms and knowledge in exchange for the formula that could transform the ordinary into the extraordinary.

Yet the Great Alchemist remained elusive. At his doorstep, he greeted them with a knowing smile and uttered the same cryptic phrase: "Gold is not what you seek."

Confusion clouded the minds of those who heard him. To them, gold symbolized wealth and power, yet to the alchemist, it was a mere metaphor—an emblem of a deeper transformation: mastery of creative excellence and the alchemy of the mind.

One day, a young man named **Elias** resolved to seek out the Great Alchemist. Unlike the others, Elias was not driven by the allure of wealth; he was captivated by the art of creation itself. Growing up, he watched his father, a humble craftsman, shape raw wood into exquisite furniture. Elias marveled at how his father transformed simple materials into elegant pieces, igniting a fire within him.

Elias's curiosity extended beyond woodwork. He spent afternoons at the village forge, mesmerized by the blacksmith's skill as he heated metal, hammering it into tools and weapons. The rhythmic clang of metal against anvil echoed in Elias's ears, and he peppered the blacksmith with questions: "How does heat change the metal? What makes it strong or weak?"

As he grew older, his attempts at crafting often fell short of his expectations. Each failed project left him frustrated, feeling as though an invisible wall separated him from the mastery he sought. Sleepless nights were spent contemplating what he was missing, aware that the spark he longed for remained elusive.

One evening, Elias overheard travelers in the village square discussing the Great Alchemist. Their words stirred something within him. "Gold is not what you seek," one traveler remarked, and Elias felt a tug at his heart. He realized that the alchemist might hold the answer to his questions about creative excellence, the key to unlocking the extraordinary from the ordinary.

Driven by insatiable curiosity, Elias decided to embark on a journey to find the Great Alchemist—not for riches but for the knowledge to create. With a simple pack and determination, he ventured toward the mountains where the alchemist's workshop lay hidden.

## Elias's Journey begins

The journey was long and treacherous, winding through dense forests where sunlight rarely touched the ground. Each step felt like a test, as if the forest were daring him to turn back. Yet Elias pressed on, fueled by the same curiosity that had always driven him.

Finally, he arrived at the workshop—an unassuming structure made of rough stone, surrounded by towering trees. For a moment, doubt crept in. Would he, too, be turned away?

He knocked on the heavy door, and after what felt like an eternity, it creaked open. The Alchemist stood there, his silver hair framing a face lined with age, yet his eyes sparkled with the vibrancy of youth.

"You are not here for gold," he stated, not as a question but as a fact.

"No," Elias replied with his voice steady and full of excitement. "I seek something much greater—the knowledge of how to create."

The alchemist's lips curled into a knowing smile. "Then let us explore together."

## The first lesson

As Elias stepped into the workshop, warmth enveloped him. The air was rich with the scent of burning wood and molten metal. Strange instruments lined the walls—beakers filled with shimmering liquids, tools he could not recognize, and metals that gleamed with colors he had never seen.

"Tell me, Elias," the alchemist began, "what do you think is the first step in creation?"

Elias paused, taken aback by the question. "I suppose it's about understanding the materials?"

"Understanding is a start," the alchemist replied. "But what fuels that understanding?"

"Curiosity," Elias stated, feeling a flicker of insight.

"**Curiosity is truly the seed of creative excellence**," the alchemist affirmed, his eyes gleaming with approval. "Now, tell me, where does that curiosity lead you?"

Elias's eyes glittered with excitement as he replied, "I want to discover how to transform the ordinary into something extraordinary."

"This is precisely why I have chosen you for this journey—no one else has been granted this opportunity," the Alchemist said, his voice filled with encouragement as he gestured toward a massive furnace in the corner. "The first step in your adventure is to place raw material into the fire."

Elias felt a surge of joy, glad to have passed this first test of courage. He realized that this moment marked the beginning of his creative journey.

## Facing the Fire

But as he gazed into the roaring flames of the furnace, the thrill of joy was quickly overshadowed by a surge of fear. "This feels so risky! What if I fail?"

"Is failure really a setback?" the alchemist challenged, raising an eyebrow. "What can it teach you about your journey?"

Elias took a moment to reflect, his thoughts racing. "It can reveal what doesn't work... and perhaps guide me toward new discoveries."

"Then you must face the fire, Elias," the alchemist urged, his voice steady and encouraging. "Embrace the risk, for that is where true transformation begins. Remember, every outstanding creation is born from the courage to take the first step, even in the face of uncertainty."

With a newfound determination, Elias stepped forward and placed the cold, lifeless metal into the furnace. As he watched it begin to glow, he felt a powerful lesson crystallizing within him: creative excellence is not about certainty; it is about daring to move forward, even when the outcome is unknown.

"**Courage is what allows curiosity to become action,**" the alchemist mused thoughtfully. "What do you believe might unfold if you fully embrace that courage in your creative endeavors?"

Elias took a deep breath, his resolve strengthening. "Maybe I'll discover new methods or ideas I hadn't even considered."

"Indeed," the alchemist affirmed with a nod. "But how do you think you can cultivate that courage within yourself?"

Elias paused, reflecting on his journey. "Perhaps by embracing each attempt, knowing that everyone brings me closer to my goal."

"Reflection is indeed powerful," the alchemist said. "Now, as you work with the metal, what will you observe?"

Elias felt a surge of confidence welling up inside. "I'll closely watch how the heat transforms it, and I'll be ready to adjust my approach as needed."

"Excellent," the alchemist smiled. "Let's see how this unfolds."

## The Power of New Ideas and Refinement

As the metal heated, Elias began to explore. He adjusted the temperature, repositioned the metal, and considered different techniques he had not tried before. Whenever he faced a challenge, he asked himself, "What fresh approach could I take?"

"Remember, creative excellence is a journey," the alchemist reminded him. "What does that mean for how you should think about your work?"

Elias pondered this. "It means I need to be open to new possibilities and not just rely on what I already know."

"Yes," the alchemist affirmed. "And what can you learn from your setbacks?"

Elias nodded thoughtfully. "They can highlight what doesn't work, guiding me to refine my ideas and methods."

As Elias explored, he embraced the rhythm of creative excellence. Each setback revealed new insights, and every small success brought him closer to his goal. The alchemist observed him, occasionally prompting Elias with questions that pushed him to think deeper.

"What patterns do you notice in your thinking?" he would ask.

"Sometimes, the metal responds well, and other times it doesn't," Elias noted. "I need to understand what influences those reactions."

"Indeed, observation is crucial. How can you apply your insights moving forward?" the alchemist encouraged.

Elias reflected. "I can analyze the variables at play, like the temperature and pressure, and consider how my ideas can adapt to achieve the desired result."

"Exactly," the alchemist said, beaming with pride. **"Cognition, then, is not just about generating ideas—**

**it's about harnessing them effectively to elevate your creative process."**

## The blacksmith's insight

Despite his growing understanding, Elias felt something was still missing. The metal never transformed into the brilliance he imagined, and frustration gnawed at him.

"Sometimes, we need the wisdom of others to see what we cannot," the alchemist suggested one evening. "Have you considered seeking insights beyond this workshop?"

Elias nodded slowly. "Yes, a blacksmith shapes metal through heat and pressure. Maybe he could help me understand what I'm missing."

Reluctantly, Elias agreed, curious yet uncertain about how a blacksmith could contribute to his journey. The next morning, he made his way to the village forge. There, he shared his struggles with the blacksmith.

Listening intently, the blacksmith examined the metal. "You're treating it too delicately. It needs force. Do not be afraid to hammer it hard," he advised.

A pang of doubt gripped Elias. "Could that really work? What if I ruin it?"

"What do you think will happen if you don't try?" the blacksmith countered, his eyes glinting with experience.

With newfound determination, Elias followed the blacksmith's advice, striking the metal with more force. To his surprise, the material responded differently, revealing its resilience. In that moment, he realized that collaboration could provide fresh perspectives he had not considered before.

Upon returning to the workshop, the alchemist observed Elias's newfound energy. "Why do you think it's important to seek insights from others?" he asked.

"Because they can see things I might miss," Elias replied. "Their experiences can guide my own explorations."

"Exactly," the alchemist nodded. "**Creative excellence flourishes in environments where diverse ideas converge.**" After a thoughtful pause, he added, "So, how will you nurture that spirit of collaboration moving forward?"

Elias thought for a moment. "I could reach out to more artisans and learn from them; maybe even work alongside them."

"Then let that be your next step," the alchemist encouraged, a glimmer of approval in his eyes.

## Overcoming Mental Barriers

Embracing a new level of intensity, Elias applied the blacksmith's advice. With each blow of the hammer, the metal began to transform from dull to radiant, reflecting a brilliance he had long sought.

For the first time, he witnessed the metamorphosis he had been chasing. The once-stubborn material now gleamed with the brilliance of gold, as if it had been waiting for this moment all along.

As he watched metal evolve, Elias recognized the breakthrough that had occurred. "I realized I was holding onto the belief that I had to be delicate," he reflected aloud. "But sometimes, strength is needed."

"Indeed," the alchemist affirmed. "What do you think this reveals about your own beliefs?"

"I see now that my fear of making mistakes limited my creative excellence," Elias admitted, nodding slowly. "I had to challenge those beliefs to unlock the potential within the material."

"**Removing conceptual blocks is essential for creative excellence**," the alchemist said thoughtfully. "What other barriers might you encounter as you continue this journey?"

Elias pondered deeply. "I suppose any assumptions I hold about how things should be done could hinder my progress."

"Exactly, the journey of creative excellence requires constant self-reflection and a willingness to challenge your own thinking."

## Perseverance and the Near Defeat

Elias continued to refine his technique, applying everything he had learned from the alchemist and the blacksmith. Yet, despite these improvements, the full transformation still eluded him. Day after day, he returned to the furnace, working tirelessly, but the brilliant gold he sought remained just out of reach. Each time he thought he was close, something would falter.

Frustration gnawed at him. One evening, after yet another failed attempt, Elias sat by the furnace, his heart heavy with defeat. "Maybe I should just give up," he said quietly.

"What makes you think that?" the alchemist asked, approaching him.

"I've tried everything. The gold remains just beyond my grasp," Elias replied, his voice thick with disappointment.

"Is that so?" the alchemist replied. "What have you learned from this journey?"

Elias pondered for a moment. "I've learned that creative excellence is a process, one filled with challenges. Each failure teaches me something."

"Then is failure truly an end?" the alchemist pressed gently.

"No," Elias admitted. "It's part of the journey."

"Then stay one more day. Keep trying. What could you learn if you persist?"

Reluctantly, Elias agreed, determined to give it one last try.

The next morning, Elias rose early, filled with renewed determination. This time, he focused on the process rather than instant success. As he approached the furnace, he allowed the work to unfold, trusting in everything he had learned.

As the hours passed, he noticed something subtle yet extraordinary happening. The metal began to glow faintly with a soft, golden light. It flickered and grew brighter as he patiently applied what he had learned.

Elias stood back, staring in awe at the furnace, his heart swelling with a mixture of disbelief and joy. The metal glowed brilliantly, shining with a hue that he had only imagined before. He had done it. After all the arduous work, all the setbacks, and all the moments of doubt, he had finally achieved the transformation he had sought for so long.

The realization washed over him slowly—he had never been as far from success as he thought. All along, the transformation had been built piece by piece, step by step. It was not about a single dramatic moment; it was about the accumulation of consistent effort.

As the flames danced in the furnace and the gold gleamed brighter than ever, Elias knew that the true secret was not in any one technique or tool. **The secret was in persistence, the patience, and the unwavering commitment to the craft.** It was in trusting the process, even when the results were not immediate.

## The Formula for Creative Excellence

After months of tireless work, countless experiments, and moments of near-defeat, Elias had finally discovered the secret—the true formula for creative excellence. As he stood before the glowing furnace, the gold shimmered in the firelight, symbolizing far more than just a physical transformation.

The real secret was neither a shortcut nor a single revelation. It lay in a profound understanding of a layered process: curiosity, which inspired him to explore every possible avenue; courage, which empowered him to take risks despite the uncertainty of the outcome; cognition, which enabled him to reflect on and refine his ideas; collaboration, through which he gained invaluable insights from the blacksmith; and the critical realization that removing conceptual blocks was essential for unlocking creative excellence. Ultimately, it was consistency—the unwavering commitment to show up each day and nurture his craft—that propelled him toward success.

As the alchemist watched Elias, he smiled knowingly. "You've found the formula," he said, his voice filled with approval and pride.

Elias nodded, finally understanding that creative excellence was not a secret to be handed down; it was a process to be lived. The journey he had undertaken transformed not only the metal but also himself.

The glow of the gold brightened the workshop, illuminating the path ahead. Elias knew this was not the end of the journey but the beginning. The formula for creative excellence was not a destination—it was a lifelong process, one he would carry with him into every endeavor, forever seeking, refining, and creating.

## Chapter 2
# Decoding the Creative Excellence Equation

At the close of the previous chapter, we unlocked the secret formula for creative excellence through the story of Elias and the Great Alchemist. As Elias's journey demonstrated, creative excellence is not a magical, one-time spark but rather a process—one that combines Curiosity, Courage, Cognition, Collaboration, and Consistency to produce something extraordinary. His discovery that removing mental barriers, or conceptual blocks, was essential to achieving creative excellence is the first key insight we take forward.

In this chapter, we will take a closer look at the Creative Excellence Equation itself, understanding each of its components as essential steps in cultivating creative excellence. Like Elias's journey, our own creative journeys are filled with moments of experimentation, persistence, and refinement. But by decoding this Equation, you will see how creative excellence can be fostered systematically—how it is possible to harness your potential through a repeatable, structured approach.

As we move forward, we will explore how this Equation can be applied in real-world contexts, not just in theoretical terms but as a practical framework that can be used by anyone, from artists to entrepreneurs, educators, and leaders. Creative excellence, as you will soon see, is within everyone's reach. Let us start by planting the seeds of curiosity and build from there as we unlock the process behind creative mastery.

Imagine a garden filled with rich, fertile soil, awaiting a seed that will one day grow into something extraordinary. Creative excellence is like this garden—it requires the right conditions, nurtured over time, to allow ideas to flourish. But it is not just any seed that will grow; it must be planted in the right way, at the right time, with the right care. Creative excellence, like any process, can be cultivated with intention and structure.

This chapter is dedicated to decoding the Creative Excellence Equation, a framework designed to show that creative excellence is not some elusive, magical event reserved for a few gifted individuals. Instead, it is a structured process that anyone can engage in. Just like planting a seed, it takes consistent care, curiosity, courage, and collaboration to achieve creative brilliance.

**Creative Excellence vs. Creativity: Key Differences**

As you have progressed through the book, you may have noticed that we consistently use the term *Creative Excellence* rather than *Creativity* to represent true creative success. Before we dive into unveiling the *Creative Excellence Equation*, it is crucial to understand the distinction between these two concepts.

While both *creativity* and *creative excellence* involve the generation of innovative ideas and solutions, the difference lies in their depth, application, and sustainability. Let us explore these key distinctions:

1. **Creativity:**
   - Creativity is the **ability** to generate original, innovative ideas or solutions. It can be spontaneous, unstructured, and exploratory.
   - It often emerges in bursts of inspiration and is seen as a natural trait or skill that can be developed over time.
   - Creativity focuses on ideation—the generation of something new or novel without necessarily considering its practical application or long-term impact.
   - It tends to be more individualistic, driven by personal imagination, artistic expression, or problem-solving in specific moments.

2. **Creative Excellence:**
   - Creative excellence is the **process** to consistently produce high-quality, impactful creative solutions that lead to transformation and measurable success. It is a blend of creativity with strategic execution, refinement, and sustainability.
   - It goes beyond just generating ideas—it includes refining, executing, and improving those ideas in a structured way to ensure real-world impact.

- Achieving creative excellence involves disciplined processes, such as feedback loops, iteration, collaboration, and learning from failure. It is about mastering the craft of creativity, turning it into a powerful tool for personal or organizational success.
- Creative excellence is often a collaborative effort, requiring input from diverse perspectives, team alignment, and continuous improvement to turn ideas into innovations that last.

In essence, *creativity* is the ability to spark current ideas, while *creative excellence* is the process of consistently cultivating, refining, and transforming those ideas into meaningful outcomes. Creative excellence combines creativity with persistence, discipline, and strategic thinking, ensuring that the creative process results in sustained innovation and lasting success.

## The Creative Excellence Equation

At its core, the Creative Excellence Equation follows a straightforward yet powerful equation:

> **Creative Excellence =**
>
> (Curiosity + Courage + Cognition + Collaboration) × Consistency/ Conceptual Block

Each element of the Creative Excellence Equation—Curiosity, Courage, Cognition, Collaboration, Consistency, and Conceptual Blocks—plays a vital role in fostering creative excellence. When these elements are combined, they create an environment that nurtures and supports creative thinking and innovation.

- **Additive Factors**: curiosity, courage, cognition, and collaboration are considered additive factors, meaning that they can enhance and compensate for one another. For example, if an individual lacks courage to pursue a new idea, their curiosity can inspire them to explore further, or collaboration with a supportive team could provide the encouragement needed to take risks. This interplay allows individuals to draw on different elements based on their current needs and circumstances.

- **Multiplicative Impact**: In contrast, consistency exerts a multiplicative impact on creative excellence. This means that consistent efforts compound over time, leading to significant and exponential growth in creative output. By continuously engaging in creative practices, individuals cultivate habits that reinforce their creative excellence, making them more resilient and adaptable in the face of challenges.

- **Divisional Impact**: Conceptual Blocks, such as fear or rigid thinking, have a divisional impact on creative excellence. These blocks can inhibit the creative process by limiting one's ability to think freely and explore new ideas. When conceptual blocks are present, they can effectively diminish the overall capacity for creative excellence, stifling innovation before it can take root.

In summary, the combination of these elements creates a dynamic system where creative excellence can flourish, emphasizing the importance of nurturing the additive factors while mitigating the effects of conceptual blocks.

## Curiosity: The Seed of Creative excellence

Curiosity is where it all begins. Just as a seed holds the potential for growth, curiosity holds the potential for creative breakthroughs. It is the driving force that makes us ask questions, explore new possibilities, and look at the world through fresh eyes.

Think of how a child approaches the world—with a sense of wonder, eager to discover how things work. That is the mindset we need to cultivate to unlock creative excellence. In the Creative Excellence Equation, curiosity is the seed that initiates the process. Without it, there is no starting point. Curiosity compels us to dig deeper, to uncover insights that others might overlook, and to seek out connections between seemingly unrelated things.

**Example**: Think about how the Wright brothers, driven by their curiosity about flight, meticulously studied birds' flight patterns before designing their aircraft. They questioned how wings created lift and applied those principles to their early designs, ultimately achieving the first controlled, powered flight in 1903. Their curiosity laid the foundation for the modern aviation industry.

## Courage: The Sunlight That Fuels Growth

If curiosity plants the seed, courage provides the sunlight necessary for growth. Creative excellence often requires us to step into the unknown, to take risks and face the possibility of failure. Without courage, even the most curious mind might hesitate to act on new ideas.

Courage in creative excellence means embracing uncertainty. It is about trying something new, knowing that it might not work out, but believing that the attempt is valuable. In this way, courage acts like sunlight, giving energy and vitality to creative efforts. Without it, the seed of curiosity would remain dormant, never becoming exposed.

**Example**: Consider J.K. Rowling's journey while writing Harry Potter. Despite facing numerous rejections from publishers, her courage to continue pursuing her vision led to the creation of one of the most successful book series in history. Rowling's willingness to take risks, despite the obstacles, was crucial to her eventual success.

## Cognition: Watering and Refining Ideas

Just as a plant needs water to grow, creative excellence needs the nourishment of cognition to flourish. Cognition refers to the mental processes that allow us to think critically, analyze, and refine our ideas. It is the part of the process where raw creative excellence is honed into something practical and actionable.

Cognition ensures that creative excellence is not just about wild, unstructured ideas—it is about shaping those ideas into something useful. It involves problem-solving, decision-making, and thoughtful refinement, turning initial sparks into fully realized concepts. This phase is crucial for weeding out impractical ideas and focusing on the ones that hold the most promise.

**Example**: Steve Jobs exemplified this aspect of creative excellence when he led the development of the iPhone. The initial idea of combining a phone, an iPod, and a web browser was simple, but Jobs and his team spent years refining the product, addressing technical challenges, and perfecting the design before it was ready for the market. Cognition was key to turning an idea into a revolutionary device.

## Collaboration: The Fertile Soil

Creative excellence thrives when it is nurtured by collaboration. Just as fertile soil provides the nutrients needed for a seed to grow, collaboration enriches the creative process by bringing in diverse perspectives. Working with others allows ideas to evolve in ways that would not be possible alone.

In the Creative Excellence Equation, collaboration plays a key role in enhancing creative excellence. It is through collaboration that we gain insights we might have missed, and our ideas are strengthened through feedback and shared experiences. Collaboration turns individual creative excellence into collective innovation, producing richer, more refined outcomes.

**Example**: Consider the success of Pixar Animation Studios. Their model of creative collaboration is one of the key reasons behind their groundbreaking films. Directors, animators, and writers work together to iterate on storylines, visuals, and character development, each contributing their unique perspective. This collaborative process results in films that consistently push the boundaries of animation.

## Consistency: The Gardener of Creative excellence

While curiosity, courage, cognition, and collaboration are critical, they can only achieve their full potential with consistency. Consistency is the gardener who shows up every day, tending to the process, ensuring that creative excellence becomes a habit.

Creative excellence is not a one-time event—it is a practice. Just as a plant needs regular care to thrive, creative excellence needs consistent effort to flourish. Without consistency, even the best ideas might wither before they reach their full potential. The Creative Excellence Equation emphasizes that creative excellence is not about waiting for the occasional flash of inspiration but about showing up, day after day, to nurture the process.

**Example**: The composer Ludwig van Beethoven is a perfect example of creative consistency. Despite being deaf later in life, he continued to compose and refine his music daily. His consistent dedication resulted in some of the most iconic symphonies ever written, including his Ninth Symphony, which was composed almost entirely without the ability to hear.

## Removing conceptual blocks: Weeding the Garden

Finally, conceptual blocks—like fear, perfectionism, and rigid thinking—act as weeds in the creative garden. If left unchecked, they can choke out creative growth, stifling the process before it even begins.

To cultivate creative excellence, we must actively work to remove these blocks. This means recognizing when fear is holding us back, when perfectionism is stopping us from acting, or when rigid thinking is preventing us from seeing new possibilities. By removing these mental barriers, we create space for creative excellence to flow freely.

**Example**: A perfect illustration of overcoming conceptual blocks is the story of Thomas Edison's invention of the light bulb. He famously failed over 1,000 times before creating a working prototype. Instead of seeing these attempts as failures, Edison reframed them as lessons on what did not work, thereby removing the block of perfectionism and fear of failure.

## The Creative Process: A Cycle, not a Moment

Creative excellence is often thought of as a moment of sudden inspiration, but the Creative Excellence Equation shows that it is actually a process—a cycle that repeats and evolves over time. Like the growth of a seed into a plant, creative excellence requires continuous nurturing, and it does not stop once a single idea has bloomed. Each creative success builds upon the last, and the process begins anew, with fresh curiosity, renewed courage, and refined cognition.

In the chapters that follow, we will explore each element of the Equation in greater depth. You will learn how to cultivate curiosity, build courage, refine your ideas through cognition, collaborate effectively, and maintain the consistency needed to make creative excellence a lasting habit. Along the way, we will also examine how to overcome the conceptual blocks that can hinder creative growth.

By embracing the Creative Excellence Equation, you'll discover that creative excellence is not an elusive gift but a skill you can practice and develop. Just like planting and tending to a garden, creative excellence requires intention, effort, and patience—but the rewards are worth it. Creative excellence becomes a lifelong practice, a way of approaching the world with curiosity, courage, and an open mind.

Let us begin our journey into the garden of creative excellence, where the seeds of ideas can grow into something extraordinary.

# Chapter 3
# Curiosity—The Spark of Creative Alchemy

*"Curiosity is the key to creativity."* - Akio Morita

In the world of creative alchemy, curiosity is the spark that ignites everything. It is the essential starting point—the tiny yet powerful force that begins the process of transformation. Without curiosity, there is no movement, no exploration, and no discovery. Just as a spark sets fire to wood, curiosity lights up the mind with questions, pushing us to explore the unknown, challenge assumptions, and seek out new possibilities.

Curiosity is the seed in the garden of creative excellence, from which all innovation blooms. Just as a plant begins with a small seed full of potential, curiosity holds the promise of growth and possibility. It sparks that first flicker of wonder, prompting the questions that stir the mind and drive exploration. Without curiosity, creative excellence remains dormant—no breakthroughs or discoveries can take root without this essential force to propel ideas forward.

Imagine the last question that kept you up at night. Was it something small, like why your phone was acting strange? Or was it something bigger, like the mysteries of the universe or the complexity of human emotions? That nagging need to seek, to explore, to discover is the very essence of curiosity. It is the driving force behind every act of creative excellence—the moment when you encounter something puzzling, and your mind craves to know more. This is the spark that ignites creative thinking.

Whether you are trying to innovate in your workplace, solve a personal problem, or embark on a passion project, curiosity is the seed that begins the journey. It is the first step from the known to the unknown, from ordinary to extraordinary. In this chapter, we will explore the science of curiosity, why it is essential to creative excellence, and how you can cultivate it. We will examine psychological theories such as the Information Gap Theory and Berlyne's Theory of Curiosity to unpack the mechanics of curiosity, explain its role in creative excellence, and provide actionable strategies to foster a more inquisitive mindset.

## The Science of Curiosity: Why We Seek the Unknown

According to George Loewenstein's Information Gap Theory, curiosity emerges when we encounter a gap between what we know and what we want to know. This gap creates a sense of cognitive discomfort that pushes us to seek information to bridge it.

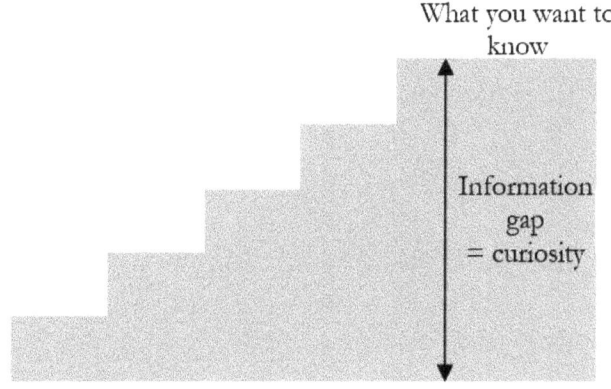

**Figure 3.1 Information Gap Theory**

Picture yourself reading a book and coming across a curious fact. You feel compelled to dig deeper, to learn more. This gap between the known and the unknown creates a drive that compels you to seek an answer. The less you know, but the more you want to know, the stronger the pull of curiosity.

On a neurological level, curiosity is linked to our brain's reward system. When we become curious, the brain releases dopamine, a neurotransmitter that motivates us to seek out latest information. The more curious we are, the more pleasurable the learning process becomes. This explains why curiosity enhances memory retention—when we are genuinely curious, we absorb and retain information better because our brain is primed for discovery.

## Types of Curiosity: Divergent vs. Focused Curiosity

Not all curiosity is the same. According to Berlyne's Theory of Curiosity, there are two types of curiosity, and both play important roles in creative excellence:

1. **Divergent Curiosity**: This form of curiosity is exploratory and open-ended. It drives us to explore new fields, learn for the sake of learning, and ask broad questions without a specific goal in mind. Divergent curiosity sparks brainstorming, creative excellence, and innovation.

   - Example: A painter experimenting with assorted styles and mediums, not to create a specific work of art but to see what new techniques might emerge.

2. **Focused Curiosity**: This is targeted curiosity, driven by a need to solve a specific problem or achieve a particular outcome. Focused curiosity helps in deep research, critical thinking, and solving complex challenges.

   - Example: A scientist investigates a single hypothesis to find a cure for a disease, focusing deeply on one problem area until it is solved.

Understanding these two types of curiosity allows you to leverage each type when needed: explore widely with divergent curiosity, then narrow your focus with concentrated curiosity when it is time to solve a problem.

## Curiosity in the Truck Industry

During my internship in the truck manufacturing industry, I had a firsthand experience that left an impression on me about the power of curiosity in driving innovation. It was an ordinary day, one of many where I shadowed my regional manager as we traveled across the region, visiting clients and production sites. But this day stood out. As we cruised down the highway, something caught my manager's eye—a brand-new truck from a competitor. I could sense a shift in his demeanor; his eyes locked onto the truck with intense focus.

Most people might have continued driving, simply acknowledging the competition, and moving on. But my manager was not like most people. He did not just glance at the truck and moved on. His curiosity was palpable, and he was not content with just a passing observation. Without hesitation, he asked the driver to pull over. I remember thinking how unusual it was to stop in the middle of our journey just to look at a competitor's truck.

As we stood beside the truck, inspecting its every detail, I saw my manager's mind at work. This was not idle curiosity or casual interest—it was the kind of curiosity that seeks to unravel mysteries, to dig deeper and uncover hidden insights. He was not simply admiring the truck; he was mentally dissecting it, comparing its features to our own models, and analyzing every curve, component, and design decision. He asked the truck driver pointed questions, wanting to understand how the truck performed, how it was received in the market, and what made it stand out.

In that moment, I realized that curiosity was not just a personality trait—it was a driving force for innovation. My manager's curiosity was not just limited to satisfying his own mind. He was looking for opportunities, searching for areas where we could improve, innovate, and outsmart the competition. It was this relentless curiosity that turned a routine drive into a moment of discovery and strategic insight.

What struck me even more was how my manager shared his thought process with me. He asked me questions too: "What do you think about this design? How does it compare to our trucks? What features could we implement in our next model?" I felt valued, included in the process of exploration. His curiosity sparked my own, and suddenly, I was not just observing the truck—I was actively engaging, thinking critically about what made it different and how we could learn from it.

That single stop on the side of the road did not just end there. The insights we gathered shaped discussions back at the office, eventually influencing changes in our product strategy. We refined our designs, tweaked our features, and stayed competitive in a tough market—all because of that moment of curiosity. It taught me a powerful lesson: innovation does not always come from groundbreaking ideas or massive research projects. Sometimes, it starts with a simple question, a desire to know more, and the willingness to act on that curiosity.

## Steve Jobs' Curiosity Revolution

Steve Jobs was famously curious, constantly asking, "What if?" —a simple yet powerful question that laid the foundation for some of the most groundbreaking innovations of our time. In the early 2000s, cell phones were cumbersome, dominated by small screens and physical keypads. These devices, while functional, limited how users interacted with technology. Jobs, driven by his innate curiosity, began questioning the conventional design. "What if we got rid of the keyboard entirely?" he wondered.

This single, revolutionary question led to the creation of the first touchscreen smartphone, which fundamentally changed not just the way we use phones but how we engage with technology. It transformed mobile devices into more than just tools for communication—they became powerful handheld computers, entertainment systems, and gateways to the digital world.

Jobs' curiosity was the initial spark, but it was his courage to challenge industry norms, his team's cognitive prowess in solving technical challenges, their collaborative innovation, and their consistent pursuit of excellence that nurtured this idea into the product we now know as the iPhone. The ripple effect of Jobs' curiosity revolutionized not just smartphones but the entire tech industry, shaping the future of how we live, work, and communicate.

## Jane Goodall's Curiosity in the Wild

Jane Goodall, one of the world's most renowned primatologists, serves as a living testament to the power of curiosity in scientific discovery. When Goodall first entered the field in the 1960s, she lacked formal scientific training—something that many people might have considered a disadvantage. Yet, what she lacked in formal education, she made up for with an unyielding curiosity about the lives and behaviors of chimpanzees. She dared to ask questions that others had not considered.

While most researchers of the time maintained a distance from their subjects, observing animals in artificial settings, Goodall immersed herself in the chimpanzees' natural environment. She spent years living among them, observing their social structures, communication methods, and daily behaviors. Her curiosity led her to question long-held beliefs about the distinction between humans and animals. One of her most famous discoveries was that chimpanzees could use tools—previously thought to be a behavior exclusive to humans.

Goodall's groundbreaking work forever changed the fields of anthropology and primatology, expanding our understanding of intelligence and behavior in the animal kingdom. Her relentless curiosity drove her to challenge existing norms, and in doing so, she opened entirely new ways of thinking about both humans and animals. Goodall's story reminds us that curiosity can fuel revolutionary scientific progress, even when it comes from an unexpected source.

## Richard Feynman and the Power of Wonder

Nobel Prize-winning physicist Richard Feynman exemplified the childlike wonder that fuels true curiosity. From an early age, Feynman was fascinated by how things worked. As a child, he would take apart radios and other household objects just to see their inner workings—an early expression of his natural curiosity about the world around him.

This same sense of wonder stayed with Feynman throughout his life, driving his pioneering work in quantum mechanics. While many in his field adhered to established theories, Feynman's insatiable curiosity led him to challenge the status quo. He asked unconventional questions that others might have dismissed as trivial or too complex. This willingness to question, explore, and experiment was central to his revolutionary contributions to physics, including his work on quantum electrodynamics, for which he won the Nobel Prize.

Feynman's life and career serve as powerful reminders that curiosity, when nurtured throughout life, can lead to extraordinary achievements. His story illustrates that the curiosity of a child—the eagerness to take things apart, to ask "why" and "how"—is not something to outgrow but something to cultivate. His relentless pursuit of understanding proves that curiosity is not only about seeking answers but about finding joy in the process of exploration itself.

## NASA's Apollo 13 Mission: Curiosity as Problem-Solving

Curiosity is not just a tool for generating new ideas—it's a vital asset for solving problems, especially in high-stakes, high-pressure situations. A striking example of this is NASA's Apollo 13 mission, a story of curiosity-driven ingenuity under life-threatening circumstances. In 1970, an explosion severely damaged the spacecraft during the mission to the moon, leaving the crew stranded in space with limited resources and no clear path home.

The engineers and astronauts could have succumbed to panic, but instead, their curiosity sparked innovation. Instead of focusing on what was lost or what they did not have, they asked, "What can we do with what we have?" This simple question opened the door to a series of creative solutions. Through a combination of resourcefulness and relentless questioning, they devised ways to make the damaged spacecraft functional enough to bring the astronauts safely back to Earth.

The Apollo 13 mission exemplifies how curiosity, paired with courage, can lead to critical problem-solving. When faced with seemingly insurmountable challenges, it was curiosity that allowed NASA's team to think outside the box, repurpose existing materials, and develop new strategies under intense pressure. This mission highlights how curiosity is not just about exploration—it's also about resilience and the ability to adapt when the stakes are at their highest.

## Key Strategies for Nurturing Creative Curiosity

Curiosity, like creative excellence, can be cultivated and developed with the right strategies. By creating environments that encourage exploration, risk-taking, and inquiry, curiosity becomes an active skill that grows over time. Here are six key strategies for nurturing creative curiosity, grounded in psychological theories and practical applications:

## 1. Encourage questioning.

One of the most effective ways to foster curiosity is by encouraging people to ask questions—especially deep, probing questions that challenge assumptions. The Socratic Method, rooted in ancient philosophy, is a powerful tool for this. Rather than providing answers, it encourages individuals to ask "why" repeatedly, digging beneath the surface of any given topic.

In The Creative Alchemy, the Alchemist utilizes Socratic questioning to guide Elias in exploring the nature of gold, prompting him to think critically about what it truly represents. By continuously asking "why," "what if," or "how," individuals are driven to explore new dimensions of a problem or idea, making them more active participants in their learning or work process.

Example: In a workplace setting, a manager might ask, "Why do we follow this process?" or "What if we tried it another way?" These questions can inspire employees to think more critically and uncover potential improvements. In education, teachers can encourage students to keep asking why something happens, pushing them to think beyond the obvious.

**Key takeaway**: Asking questions keeps the mind engaged and open to innovative ideas, turning curiosity into a habit that continually deepens understanding and fosters innovation.

## 2. Provide Freedom to Explore

Autonomy is a critical factor in nurturing curiosity. **Self-Determination Theory (SDT)** emphasizes that individuals are more motivated to explore when they have control over their work and decisions. When people are given the freedom to pursue their interests, curiosity flourishes as they take ownership of their learning and creative process.

Providing this autonomy means allowing individuals to follow their instincts, experiment with current ideas, and venture outside of conventional boundaries. It fosters an environment where curiosity thrives because there is no fear of doing things "the wrong way."

Example: Google famously allows employees to spend 20% of their time on projects of their choice. This freedom has led to the development of some of Google's most innovative products, including Gmail. Similarly, teachers can let students choose topics for projects, giving them more control and motivation to dive deeply into areas that intrigue them.

**Key takeaway**: By giving people the freedom to explore on their own terms, you allow curiosity to blossom, leading to more creative outcomes and sustained interest.

## 3. Embrace Ambiguity

Ambiguity is often seen as uncomfortable, but it can be a powerful driver of curiosity. **Tolerance for Ambiguity** refers to one's ability to remain open and curious even when things are unclear or uncertain. Ambiguity naturally sparks curiosity, as it pushes individuals to ask questions and explore different possibilities.

When people are faced with uncertainty, they are compelled to seek clarity, which drives them to be more creative and resourceful. Encouraging environments that leave room for open-ended questions and challenges can fuel this process.

Example: A software development team tasked with creating a new product may receive only a vague outline of the project's goals. The ambiguity of the task forces them to explore various solutions, think outside the box, and approach the problem from different angles, leading to innovative outcomes.

**Key takeaway**: By embracing ambiguity, you encourage a mindset of exploration and discovery, where curiosity is the force that drives people to seek solutions in unfamiliar territories.

## 4. Reward Exploration

In many professional or educational settings, rewards are often tied to the outcome. However, to foster curiosity, it's essential to reward the process of exploration, not just the end results. **Intrinsic Motivation Theory**, developed by Deci and Ryan, suggests that when people are motivated by internal rewards, such as the satisfaction of learning or discovering something new, they are more likely to engage in curiosity-driven behavior.

By acknowledging and celebrating the act of exploration—whether it leads to success or not—you reinforce the value of curiosity. This, in turn, encourages individuals to stay curious, keep experimenting, and push boundaries, even when the outcome is uncertain.

Example: During performance reviews, a company could highlight an employee's effort to explore recent technologies or processes, even if the results were not immediately impactful. By focusing on the process of exploration rather than just success, curiosity is recognized as an ongoing and valuable pursuit.

**Key takeaway**: Rewarding the act of exploration motivates individuals to continue asking questions and taking creative risks, sustaining curiosity as a habit.

## 5. Set constraints to foster creative excellence.

While freedom is essential for curiosity, constraints can fuel it by forcing individuals to think more creatively. **The Paradox of Constraints** suggests that setting boundaries, whether they be time, resources, or materials, can stimulate curiosity and innovation by pushing people to find solutions within limitations.

When constraints are introduced, people are compelled to think outside the box, make connections they might not have otherwise considered, and find resourceful solutions. This encourages curiosity by creating a challenge that requires exploration within the given framework.

Example: A design team might be tasked with creating a product using only a limited budget or a specific set of materials. The constraints force the team to innovate and get curious about how to maximize the use of their resources. In education, a teacher might give students a time limit for a creative project, pushing them to make quick decisions and explore efficient methods.

**Key takeaway:** Setting constraints can actually enhance curiosity by forcing people to think more deeply and resourcefully, leading to creative breakthroughs.

By incorporating these strategies—encouraging questioning, providing autonomy, embracing ambiguity, supporting risk-taking, rewarding exploration, and setting constraints—you create an environment where curiosity can thrive. These practices not only enhance individual curiosity but also help foster a culture of innovation and creative problem-solving across teams and organizations.

Curiosity, when nurtured in the right way, becomes the driving force behind continuous learning, discovery, and creative excellence, leading to groundbreaking ideas and long-term success.

### Fostering Curiosity: Practical Exercises

To actively nurture curiosity, try incorporating these exercises into your daily life:

- Encourage Questioning: Keep asking questions, especially "why" and "what if?" This drives deeper thinking and pushes you to explore beyond the obvious.

Example: In a business meeting, ask, "Why do we follow this process?" or "What if we tried it differently?" These questions can open new perspectives and reveal hidden opportunities.

- Explore New Fields: Spend time learning something unrelated to your current work or interests. Curiosity thrives when we expose ourselves to unfamiliar knowledge and experiences.

Example: A software developer might take up painting or study history, which could inspire new ways of thinking in their own field.

- Reframe Problems: When you encounter a challenge, reframe the problem by asking, "What if there were no limitations?" This often leads to new solutions and approaches that weren't visible before.

Example: Instead of focusing on budget constraints for a project, ask what you would do if the budget were unlimited, then find ways to creatively apply that vision within your real constraints.

- Set Constraints to Spark Creative excellence: Paradoxically, setting constraints can fuel creative excellence by forcing you to think more deeply and resourcefully.

Example: A design team tasked with creating a product using limited materials might discover innovative solutions they would not have considered without constraints.

- Be a Beginner Again: Try learning a new hobby or skill. Approaching something as a beginner reawakens your sense of curiosity and helps you see the world with fresh eyes.

Example: Learning to play a musical instrument or a new language can spark curiosity and help you apply this fresh mindset to other areas of your life.

## Conclusion: Curiosity as the Gateway to Creative Excellence

Curiosity is the seed that ignites creative excellence. It pushes us beyond the familiar and encourages us to explore, ask questions, and imagine new possibilities. In the Creative Excellence Equation, curiosity fuels the next stages—courage, cognition, collaboration, and consistency.

In the following chapter, we will explore how courage empowers us to break through the fear of failure, embrace risk, and move forward on our creative journey. Just as curiosity sparks the desire to explore, courage fuels the determination to act.

## Chapter 4
## Courage—The Fuel of Creative Alchemy

*"Creativity takes courage."* Henri Matisse

In the journey of creative alchemy, courage is the fuel that turns sparks of inspiration into flames of action. While curiosity ignites the creative process, it is courage that sustains the fire, propelling you forward through the challenges, uncertainties, and risks that inevitably arise. Courage does not mean the absence of fear—it means having the strength and resolve to act despite the fear. It is what pushes you to venture into the unknown, to experiment with bold ideas, and to face the possibility of failure.

Courage allows you to embrace vulnerability in the creative process. Whether it is sharing an untested idea, risking rejection, or pursuing a path that others might not understand, courage empowers you to persist. It is the internal force that drives resilience, helping you to overcome setbacks and push through the obstacles that might otherwise extinguish your creative flame.

In essence, courage transforms curiosity into real-world results. It fuels the leap from imagining possibilities to pursuing them, from thinking to doing. Without courage, curiosity would remain just a fleeting thought, but with it, you push boundaries, take risks, and create something meaningful. Courage, then, is the critical ingredient that moves you from inspiration to action, transforming creative sparks into powerful flames of innovation.

Imagine you have just planted a seed of curiosity, and it's beginning to sprout. The excitement of a new idea fills you with possibilities, but soon enough, doubt creeps in: What if this idea fails? What if it is not good enough? What if others criticize it? Just as a plant needs sunlight to grow, your idea needs courage to thrive. Without sunlight, the plant withers; without courage, even the most promising ideas remain dormant. Courage is the sunlight that nurtures creative excellence. It does not banish the darkness of uncertainty but empowers you to push forward despite it.

In this chapter, we will delve into the nature of creative courage, using the alchemy framework to explore how courage transforms raw ideas into tangible outcomes. You will discover five key strategies for nurturing creative courage, each presented with real-world examples, actionable tips, and reflection exercises to help you build the resilience to carry your creative endeavors forward.

## Courage as the Sunlight of Creative Alchemy

Just as plants seek the sun, your creative ideas need courage to grow and blossom. Courage is the life-giving force that helps you overcome obstacles, face criticism, and step into the unknown. It is the essential energy that keeps the creative process alive, even in the face of fear and uncertainty.

Creative courage does not mean the absence of fear—it means moving forward in spite of it. Whether you are launching a business, composing music, or proposing a bold idea at work, courage requires you to step into vulnerability. It is about daring to expose your thoughts, your work, and yourself to the world, knowing that rejection and failure are possibilities. Like an alchemist facing unpredictable reactions in the lab, you must be willing to experiment, risk failure, and persist through the process of transformation.

Welby Altidor, in his book Creative Courage, describes vulnerability as an essential part of creative excellence. He notes that the most innovative ideas come from those willing to put themselves and their work on the line. Thomas Edison echoed this sentiment when he famously said, "I have not failed. I've just found 10,000 ways that won't work." Edison's success did not come from avoiding failure, but from his courage to persist despite it.

Stepping out of your **comfort zone**—the place of safety and predictability—is where creative growth begins. As in alchemy, the transformation process requires intense energy, pressure, and sometimes discomfort. Just as a seedling pushes through the soil to reach the sunlight, your creative excellence will thrive when you engage with the unknown, embrace uncertainty, and lean into risk.

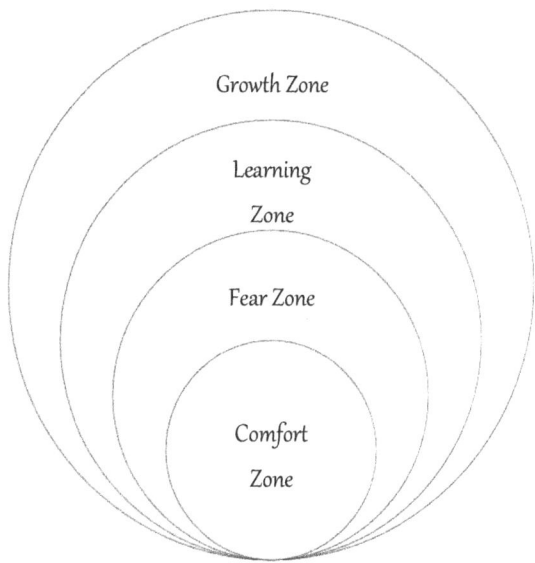

*Figure 4.1 Growth Zone Framework*

## Personal Example: Courage in Action: Creating a Unique Production Line

In my career, I have learned that courage in creative excellence isn't always about making a giant leap into the unknown; sometimes, it's about taking a deliberate, thoughtful risk in the face of uncertainty. One such moment came when I was tasked with setting up a new product line for a multinational company. It was an opportunity to do something unique, but it also came with immense pressure. The company had an established, tried-and-tested production process. The safe, logical choice was to replicate that existing line. It was familiar, comfortable, and known to deliver results within expected parameters.

But something in me hesitated. I could not shake the feeling that simply copying the standard line was not enough. I had observed inefficiencies in the current setup, and I felt a pull—an instinct—to try something different. It was one of those pivotal moments when curiosity sparked an idea, but courage was required to bring it to life.

I suggested we create a completely new, cellular manufacturing line—a radical departure from the traditional approach. It was risky. We were facing tight timelines, budget constraints, and an industry that thrived on consistency rather than experimentation. The decision weighed heavily on me. What if it did not work? What if we missed the deadlines? What if we lost money, or worse, damaged my reputation within the company?

As the doubt settled in, the stakes became clear. The easy path was to follow the established processes, but deep down, I knew this was an opportunity to push boundaries and drive innovation. I leaned into that discomfort and took the leap, guided by both analysis and instinct.

At first, there were moments of hesitation. Stakeholders were nervous, and I questioned my decision more than once. But the turning point came when I decided to break the project into smaller, manageable tests. We implemented incremental changes to see how they would perform. Every small success fueled the next step, building momentum and confidence.

The emotional highs and lows of this journey were intense. Each small victory brought a surge of hope, but each new obstacle rekindled the doubt. Yet, through it all,

I learned that courage was not about silencing fear—it was about acting despite it. Every time we faced a hurdle, I reminded myself of the bigger picture—the innovation that could come if we succeeded.

And succeed we did. The new cellular line exceeded all expectations. Not only did we meet our timelines and stay within budget, but the line also outperformed traditional setups. What began as a risky, nerve-wracking experiment became a benchmark within the industry. It was a triumph not just of innovation but of having the courage to step beyond the safety of the known into the uncertainty of the new.

The emotional impact of this experience stayed with me. Courage is not just a mental decision—it is a deeply personal journey of grappling with fear, doubt, and uncertainty. It is the emotional resilience that allows you to push through when you are tempted to retreat. In my case, it was the drive to make something better, to innovate, that overpowered the fear of failure. That emotional determination was as crucial to our success as any technical expertise or strategic planning.

This example serves as a reminder that courage in creative excellence often comes in the form of measured risks and incremental steps toward bold innovation. It is the courage to believe in a vision, to face emotional and professional challenges head-on, and to persist when the path ahead is uncertain. This was my lesson in balancing courage with curiosity, and it is a principle I carry with me in every creative endeavor.

## Courage in Action: Inspiring Real- World Examples

**Marie Curie** exemplified remarkable courage in the male-dominated field of science. Her pioneering research into radioactivity despite the unknown dangers of handling such materials transformed physics and medicine. Curie became the first woman to win a Nobel Prize and remains the only person to win Nobel Prizes in two scientific fields—physics and chemistry. Her determination to continue her work, even in the face of skepticism, societal barriers, and personal risk, speaks to the immense courage required to push scientific boundaries.

Curie's story shows that pushing the boundaries of knowledge often requires confronting personal and professional risks, but it is this courage that leads to groundbreaking discoveries.

**Elon Musk's** bold vision for **SpaceX** was seen as nearly impossible in 2002. Determined to make space exploration more affordable and accessible, Musk faced years of launch failures, financial losses, and public skepticism. However, his courage to persist through these setbacks paid off when SpaceX became the first privately funded company to send a spacecraft to the International Space Station and successfully land reusable rockets.

Musk's relentless belief in his vision revolutionized the aerospace industry, showing that creative courage can lead to industry-shifting innovations, even when the odds are stacked against success.

**Lin-Manuel Miranda's Hamilton** redefined the boundaries of Broadway, blending hip-hop with American history in a way that had never been done before. Despite skepticism from critics who doubted whether such a non-traditional approach could resonate with Broadway's typically conventional audiences, Miranda pressed forward. His courage to pursue his vision—complete with a diverse cast and modern storytelling—created a cultural phenomenon that earned 11 Tony Awards and a Pulitzer Prize for Drama.

**Lesson**: Miranda's creative leap proves that taking bold risks, even in established fields, can lead to transformative success.

## Five Key Strategies for Nurturing Creative Courage

Creative courage is an alchemical force that transforms ideas into reality. Below are five strategies to nurture this courage, framed through the lens of creative alchemy. Each strategy is supported by psychological theory, real-life examples, and actionable steps to help you nurture the courage that sustains creative excellence.

## 1. Create a Psychologically Safe Environment—The Crucible for Ideas

Just as alchemists needed safe, controlled environments to experiment and create, creative excellence needs a **psychologically safe environment** where ideas can flourish. **Psychological safety**, a concept developed by Amy Edmondson, fosters open communication and risk-taking by ensuring that individuals feel free to share ideas without fear of judgment or criticism. In a safe environment, creative courage can blossom as people feel empowered to take risks.

Imagine a laboratory where every reaction is a learning opportunity rather than a mistake to be avoided. In the same way, a team that feels safe to experiment and fail will generate more daring and innovative ideas.

**Strategy**: Cultivate an open, non-judgmental space where ideas are welcomed, and mistakes are treated as part of the learning process.

**Actionable Tip**: Hold regular "alchemy sessions" where ideas—no matter how unrefined—are shared freely. Encourage experimentation by rewarding the effort, not just the outcome.

**Reflection Exercise**: Think about a time when you hesitated to share an idea. What fears held you back? How could a more supportive environment have helped you express your thoughts more freely?

Example: Google's "Project Aristotle" revealed that teams with prominent levels of psychological safety consistently outperformed others. In these teams, creative risks led to groundbreaking innovations because individuals felt secure enough to experiment.

## 2. Face Your Fears: Fear-Setting—The Alchemist's Shield

Fear is the shadow that often clouds creative excellence, threatening to snuff out the light of courage. In alchemy, fear of failure or unintended results could stop an experiment before it even began. But just as an alchemist would face these risks, you can confront your fears through **fear-setting**, a technique championed by Tim Ferriss. Instead of letting fear control your actions, fear-setting allows you to define and mitigate your fears in a structured way, much like an alchemist carefully planning each step of an experiment.

Fear-setting helps reduce the power of fear by identifying worst-case scenarios and developing a plan to manage them.

**Strategy**: Break down your fears into manageable pieces and create a plan to address each worst-case scenario. This reduces fear's power over you and gives you the confidence to act.

**Actionable Tip**: Write down the worst possible outcomes of a creative project you are considering, and then list the steps you could take to minimize those risks. This process, like the alchemist's detailed preparation, helps you feel more in control of uncertain outcomes.

**Reflection Exercise**: What is one creative project or idea you've been avoiding because of fear? Write down the worst-case scenarios and a plan for handling them.

**Example:** When Steve Jobs developed the iPhone, he confronted the fear of market failure by assessing risks and planning for contingencies. His courage to move forward with an innovative design, despite industry skepticism, revolutionized mobile technology.

## 3. Build Courage Through Incremental Risk-Taking: The Gradual Refinement

Courage does not have to come in huge, dramatic leaps. In alchemy, transformations often happen through gradual refinement—small, incremental changes that lead to major breakthroughs. In psychology, this is supported by **Risk-Taking Propensity Theory**, which shows that we can build tolerance for risk over time by starting with smaller, manageable challenges. Like an alchemist fine-tuning a formula, you can gradually build your creative courage by taking smaller risks first.

One key to achieving creative excellence is through *incremental steps*—using prototypes, minimum viable products (MVPs), or beta launches to test ideas, mitigate risk, and learn through the process. These smaller, controlled steps allow you to refine your ideas in real-world settings, gathering feedback and making necessary adjustments without the pressure of large-scale failure. Like an alchemist testing formula before finalizing the transformation, this approach ensures that creativity evolves into practical, impactful results over time.

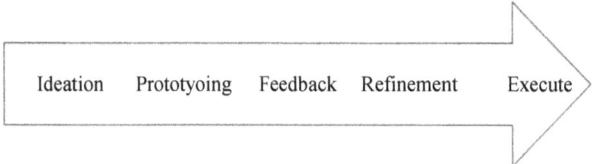

**Strategy**: Start with small, manageable risks to build confidence, then gradually increase the stakes as you become more comfortable with risk-taking.

**Actionable Tip**: Create a "ladder of challenges" where each creative task involves slightly more risk than the last. Over time, as your courage strengthens, you will be prepared for bigger challenges.

**Reflection Exercise**: What is a small creative risk you can take this week? How can you gradually increase the stakes over time?

Example: When tasked with creating a new product line at a multinational company, I began with small tests and incremental changes. As we gained confidence, we scaled up the risk, eventually creating a benchmark-setting production line.

## 4. Embrace a Growth Mindset: Reframing Failures as Opportunities—The Philosopher's Stone

In alchemy, failure is not the end but part of the transformation process. The **Growth Mindset Theory**, developed by Carol Dweck, teaches us to see failure not as a final defeat but as a necessary step toward success. Like an alchemist refining material to produce gold, a growth mindset encourages you to view each failure as an opportunity to gain experience and grow.

**Strategy**: Reframe failure as part of the creative process. Teach yourself (and others) that failure is not an endpoint but a steppingstone toward creative breakthroughs.

**Actionable Tip**: Hold "fail forward" sessions where you discuss what went wrong in a project and how to improve. This normalizes failure and reduces the fear of taking creative risks.

**Reflection Exercise**: Think of a time when you failed. What did you learn from that experience? How did it help you in your next creative endeavor?

**Example:** Pixar's creative team uses failure as a learning tool, encouraging employees to "fail early, fail often."

This philosophy has led to some of their most innovative films, including Toy Story and Inside Out.

## 5. Cultivate Resilience: The Power of Perseverance

Resilience is the ability to bounce back from setbacks and persist in the face of challenges. This concept is supported by the psychological resilience theory, which emphasizes the importance of adaptability and mental toughness in overcoming obstacles. In creative pursuits, cultivating resilience allows individuals to face failures and rejections without losing confidence in their abilities.

**Strategy:** Foster an environment that values perseverance and teaches individuals to view challenges as opportunities for growth rather than as insurmountable barriers.

**Actionable Tip:** Implement "resilience workshops" where participants engage in activities that strengthen their coping mechanisms, such as problem-solving exercises, role-playing scenarios, and group discussions about past challenges and how they overcame them.

**Reflection Exercise:** Think about a significant challenge you faced. How did your resilience help you overcome it? What strategies did you use to stay motivated?

Example: J.K. Rowling faced numerous rejections before publishing Harry Potter, yet her resilience and determination to keep pursuing her passion ultimately led to her success as a bestselling author.

## Strengthening Your Creative Courage: Practical Exercises

Creative courage is the key to overcoming fear, embracing uncertainty, and taking risks in the pursuit of innovation. To help you build and strengthen this essential trait, here are some practical exercises that will guide you in consistently taking bold actions, allowing your creative ideas to flourish.

These exercises are designed to help you gradually strengthen your creative courage by encouraging small, meaningful risks, confronting fears, and reframing failure as a positive learning experience. Courage is not something that happens overnight; it is a skill that grows through consistent practice and deliberate action. By regularly stepping outside your comfort zone, challenging your fears, and embracing vulnerability, you will develop the kind of courage that turns creative ideas into reality.

### 1. The Comfort Zone Challenge

**Objective:** Push beyond your comfort zone by engaging in activities that make you feel uncomfortable or uncertain. By doing so, you build resilience and the courage to face creative risks. **Exercise:** Set a goal to do one thing each week that challenges your comfort zone. These activities should be slightly unfamiliar or difficult, but achievable. For instance, if you usually avoid presenting new ideas, make it a goal to share one in your next team meeting. If you typically work independently, try collaborating with someone new. **Follow-up:** Reflect on how you felt before, during, and after the activity. What fears or hesitations did you experience? How did stepping outside your comfort zone enhance your confidence for future creative risks?

## 2. Fear-Setting Exercise

**Objective:** Confront your fears by visualizing worst-case scenarios and developing actionable plans to manage them. **Exercise:** Select a creative project or idea you have been avoiding due to fear. Write down the worst outcomes that could happen if you pursued it. Next, outline the steps you would take to handle these outcomes. By clearly defining your fears and addressing them, you take away their power. **Follow-up:** Revisit your fear-setting plan when faced with new challenges. Remind yourself that even the worst-case scenario is manageable, which will make you feel more empowered to act on your creative ideas.

## 3. Failure Celebration Journal

**Objective:** Reframe failure as a learning experience by documenting and celebrating it. **Exercise:** Begin a journal where you track every creative risk you have taken, focusing especially on those that did not go as planned. For each "failure," write down what you learned and how you can apply that knowledge moving forward.

This exercise shifts your perspective, helping you see failure as a necessary step in the creative process. **Follow-up:** Regularly revisit your journal to reflect on how each setback contributed to your growth. Over time, you will start to celebrate failures as steppingstones to success, which will bolster your courage to take on larger creative challenges.

## 4. The Courage Countdown

**Objective:** Bypass hesitation by counting down from 5 to 1 and taking immediate action. **Exercise:** When you feel hesitation about pursuing a creative idea—whether it is starting a new project, sharing a bold suggestion, or trying something different—count down from 5 to 1 and take immediate action. This simple countdown technique helps bypass overthinking and creates a habit of courageous action. **Follow-up:** Keep track of the moments when you used the countdown method. Over time, note how it reduces procrastination and increases your willingness to act quickly and decisively on creative opportunities.

## Conclusion: Courage as the Sunlight of Creative Alchemy

Courage is the sunlight that nurtures the seeds of creative excellence, enabling them to grow despite the shadows of fear, failure, and doubt. Creative courage is not an innate gift but a skill you can develop through consistent practice and reflection. With each step forward, you refine your ability to face challenges, take risks, and turn creative ideas into tangible outcomes.

In the next chapter, we will explore how cognition, like water, refines creative excellence by helping us shape and perfect our ideas into actionable solutions.

# Chapter 5
# Cognition—The Crucible of Creative Alchemy

*"Creativity is seeing what everyone else has seen and thinking what no one else has thought." Albert Einstein*

In the alchemy of creative excellence, if curiosity is the spark and courage is the fuel, then cognition is the crucible where the real magic happens. It is the place where raw ideas take shape, transforming from abstract thoughts into something tangible. In this mental crucible, creative excellence is refined, tested, and forged into actionable ideas. Just as a blacksmith hammers metal into form in the heat of the forge, cognition is where concepts are shaped, evaluated, and honed into something meaningful and innovative. It is the process where thoughts collide, merge, and evolve into solutions, strategies, and breakthroughs. Without the crucible of cognition, even the boldest ideas remain unformed, waiting for the mental rigor that brings them to life.

In the previous chapters, we explored how curiosity is the seed of creative excellence, planting the initial idea, and how courage acts as sunlight, providing the energy to nurture those ideas and sustain their growth. Now, we turn to cognition, the mental process that structures, organizes, and refines those ideas. Cognition provides the clarity, flexibility, and nourishment needed to help creative excellence take shape and develop into something tangible.

In the metaphor of creative garden, cognition plays the vital role of water—fluid, adaptable, and essential for growth. Just as plants rely on water to take in nutrients and develop, our creative ideas rely on cognition to transform from raw, unstructured thoughts into meaningful outcomes. Water provides balance, flexibility, and direction, and so does cognition in the creative process.

Cognition is the water that gives life to the garden of ideas. Like water that nourishes plants, cognition nourishes our creative sparks and allows them to grow into fully formed, actionable solutions. Without cognition, creative excellence would remain abstract, unfocused, and chaotic—much like a seed left without water, full of potential but never realizing it.

Cognition allows us to engage in **divergent thinking** (where ideas flow freely and without judgment) and **convergent thinking** (where those ideas are evaluated, refined, and selected). It is this balance of exploration and focus that allows creative excellence to thrive.

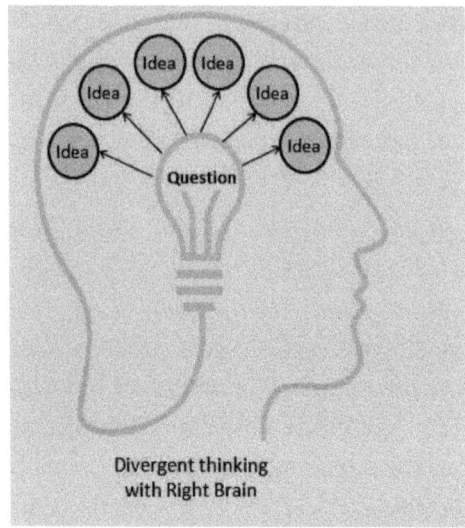

*Fig. 5.1a: Convergent and Divergent Thinking*

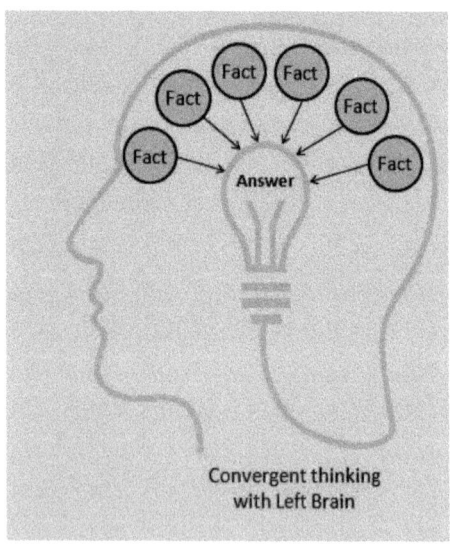

*Fig. 5.1b: Convergent and Divergent Thinking*

In this chapter, we will explore how cognition—like water—fuels the growth of ideas through divergent and convergent thinking, guiding the creative process to move fluidly between open-ended exploration and structured refinement. We will also delve into the cognitive theories that underpin creative excellence and provide practical exercises to help you harness the power of cognition in your own creative pursuits.

## Cognition as Water: The Essential Nourishment for Creative excellence

Water is a fundamental element in the growth of any plant. Without water, the seed planted by curiosity and the sunlight provided by courage would not be enough to sustain life. Similarly, cognition is the essential element that helps creative excellence grow. It provides clarity, nourishment, and refinement, allowing ideas to evolve into something real and actionable.

Cognition is fluid and adaptable, much like water. It moves freely between different states—between divergent thinking (exploring possibilities) and convergent thinking (focusing and refining those possibilities). Just as water can flow freely in a river or be directed through irrigation to nourish crops, cognition can flow freely during brainstorming sessions or be channeled into structured problem-solving processes.

Let us first explore **divergent thinking**, the process where cognition flows freely, allowing creative excellence to expand in multiple directions.

## Divergent Thinking: The Flow of Ideas

Divergent thinking is the phase of creative excellence where the mind expands, generating a wide array of possibilities. It is the cognitive process that encourages us to explore new angles, break away from conventional thinking, and push the boundaries of what we believe is possible. In this phase, cognition acts like a river, flowing freely and nourishing the creative process by allowing ideas to move in all directions.

Psychologist **J.P. Guilford** popularized the concept of divergent thinking as a core component of creative excellence. Divergent thinking involves **flexibility** (the ability to generate multiple, varied ideas), **originality** (capacity to come up with unique or novel ideas), and **fluency** (the ability to generate a large number of ideas). This process is essential for creative excellence because it allows us to open our minds and explore possibilities that we might not have considered otherwise.

Divergent thinking is like the flow of water through a landscape, reaching every part of the ground and providing nourishment to different areas. It allows us to generate a flood of ideas without worrying about whether those ideas are immediately practical or feasible.

## Example: Tesla's Electric Vehicles:

When Tesla first entered the electric vehicle (EV) market, they did not approach it by trying to fit electric components into existing gasoline-powered designs, which is what most automakers had been doing. Instead, Tesla's engineers used **divergent thinking** to re-imagine what a car could be if it were built entirely around electric propulsion.

This kind of thinking allowed them to break free from traditional automotive design principles and explore new possibilities, such as high-performance electric motors, autonomous driving capabilities, and over-the-air software updates. Tesla's success in revolutionizing the automotive industry was made possible by allowing their creative excellence to flow freely, much like water, without being constrained by the limitations of conventional thinking.

Tesla's approach to EV design exemplifies how divergent thinking allows for innovation. By letting their creative excellence flow in multiple directions, they were able to explore new possibilities and eventually develop groundbreaking solutions that disrupted the entire industry.

**Convergent thinking: structuring ideas for growth**

While divergent thinking allows ideas to flow freely, **convergent thinking** is where those ideas are refined and focused. Convergent thinking is the cognitive process of analyzing, evaluating, and narrowing down possibilities to select the best options. It is the phase where we apply logic, structure, and decision-making to turn creative ideas into practical, actionable solutions.

In the creative process, convergent thinking acts like a well-controlled irrigation system, directing water to the places where it is needed most. It ensures that ideas do not remain scattered or abstract but are channeled into structured plans that can be implemented in the real world.

**J.P. Guilford** also identified convergent thinking as a key part of creative excellence, noting that it involves **critical evaluation**, **problem solving**, and **decision-making**. Convergent thinking is what allows us to take the flood of ideas generated during divergent thinking and narrow them down to the best, most feasible options.

## Example: Apple and the Development of the iPhone:

The development of the iPhone is a prime example of how convergent thinking is used to refine creative ideas into groundbreaking products. In the pilot stages of development, Apple's engineers and designers generated a wide range of possibilities through divergent thinking, exploring unique features and designs. They considered ideas like physical keyboards, stylus inputs, and distinct types of user interfaces.

However, it was through **convergent thinking**—applying critical analysis, testing different designs, and focusing on simplicity—that they made key decisions that would define the iPhone. One of the most important decisions was to eliminate the physical keyboard, which was a standard feature in smartphones at the time, and instead use a touchscreen interface. This decision, guided by convergent thinking, became one of the defining features of the iPhone and revolutionized the smartphone industry.

Just as water can be directed to nourish specific areas of a plant, convergent thinking focuses creative energy on the most promising ideas, ensuring that they are developed into actionable solutions.

## The Iterative Loop: Balancing Divergent and Convergent Thinking

One of the key aspects of cognition as water is its ability to move fluidly between divergent and convergent thinking. Creative excellence thrives on the balance between these two processes—exploring possibilities and then refining them into workable solutions.

This iterative loop between divergent and convergent thinking is what allows creative excellence to flow freely while also ensuring that it leads to meaningful outcomes. Just as water can flow in different directions but eventually needs to be channeled to nourish plants, creative excellence needs both expansive exploration and focused refinement to be truly effective.

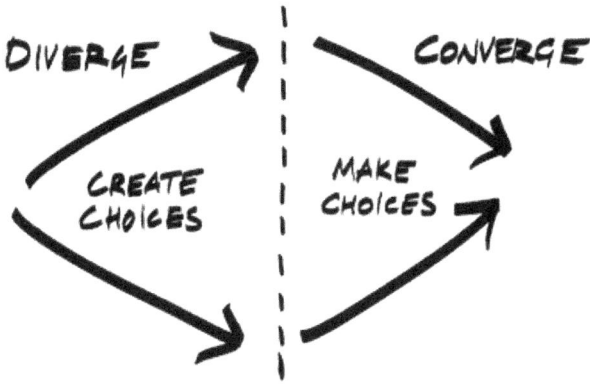

*Fig. 5.2: Complementary nature of Convergent and Divergent Thinking*

## Example: The Wright Brothers and Powered Flight:

The Wright Brothers' success in achieving powered flight is an excellent example of the iterative loop between divergent and convergent thinking. Initially, they engaged in **divergent thinking**, exploring a wide range of possibilities by studying birds in flight, experimenting with different wing shapes, and testing various control mechanisms.

However, it was through **convergent thinking** that they were able to refine their ideas and focus on developing a practical solution. They analyzed the data from their experiments, narrowed down their options, and eventually developed the **three-axis control system**, which allowed for stable and controlled flight. By moving fluidly between divergent and convergent thinking, they were able to achieve a groundbreaking technological feat that revolutionized transportation.

This balance between exploration and refinement is essential for any creative process. It allows the free flow of ideas while ensuring that those ideas are developed into actionable solutions.

## Supporting Theories: How Cognitive Nourishes Creative excellence

Cognition is at the core of the creative process, shaping and refining ideas through various cognitive models and theories. These theories provide insight into how cognition acts as the water that nourishes creative excellence, allowing it to grow and evolve.

## 1. Geneplore Model (Finke, Ward, and Smith)

The **Geneplore Model** divides the creative process into two main stages: **generation** and **exploration**. During the generation phase, ideas are generated divergently , much like water spreading across a landscape. In the exploration phase, those ideas are refined and developed, narrowing down the possibilities and focusing on specific outcomes.

This model emphasizes the **iterative loop** between divergent and convergent thinking, showing how cognition moves fluidly between these two phases. Just as water moves between states—evaporating, condensing, and flowing—cognition moves between the generation of ideas and their refinement.

## 2. Dual Process Theory (Kahneman)

**Daniel Kahneman's Dual Process Theory** highlights two systems of thinking: **System 1** (fast, intuitive thinking) and **System 2** (slow, deliberate thinking). System 1 is associated with divergent thinking, where ideas flow freely and without much conscious effort. System 2 is linked to convergent thinking, where we apply logic, analysis, and careful consideration to refine those ideas.

Cognitive flow flows like water between these two systems, ensuring that creative excellence is both expansive and focused. By balancing intuitive insights with deliberate reasoning, we can ensure that creative excellence leads to practical and meaningful outcomes.

## Insight Theory (The Aha! Moment)

**Insight theory** focuses on the moment of sudden realization—often called the "Aha!" moment—when a creative solution becomes clear. This moment of insight often comes after a period of divergent thinking where ideas are explored freely, followed by a period of convergence, where the brain processes and refines those ideas in the background.

Much like water gradually nourishing a plant until it suddenly blooms, cognition allows ideas to incubate and grow until they reach a point of clarity and insight.

## Practical Applications: Nurturing Creative excellence with Cognition

Cognition, as the water of creative excellence, can be cultivated and directed through specific techniques and practices. These exercises will help you harness the power of cognition to nourish and refine your creative ideas.

### 1. Mind Mapping for Divergent Thinking

**Objective**: Use mind mapping to explore multiple angles and possibilities.

**Exercise**: Start with a single problem or idea and create a mind map, branching out into related concepts, questions, and possibilities. Do not worry about whether the ideas are practical focus on generating as many ideas as possible.

*The Creative Alchemy*

**Follow-up**: Reflect on the connections you made and

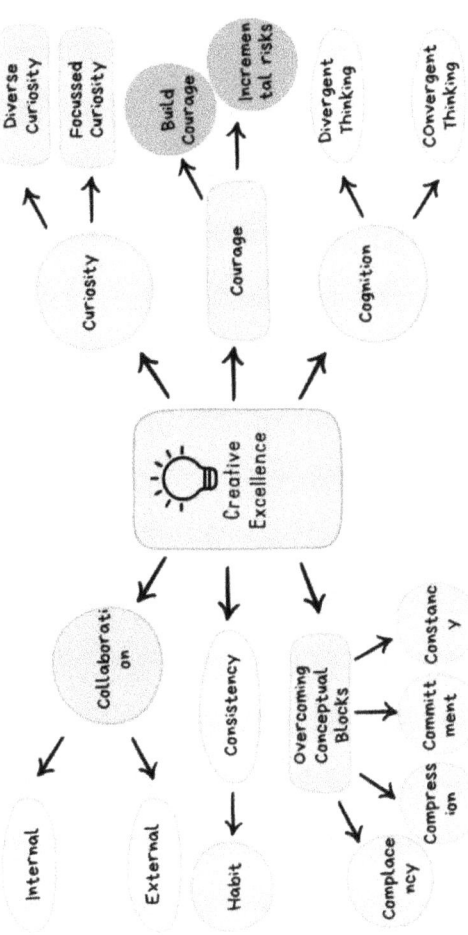

identify any surprising insights. How can you use those insights to explore new possibilities?

*Fig. 5.3: Example of a Mind Map for Creative Excellence*

## 2. Decision Matrix for Convergent Thinking

**Objective**: Use a decision matrix to evaluate and refine ideas.

**Exercise**: After brainstorming ideas, create a decision matrix with evaluation criteria such as feasibility, impact, and cost. Score each idea based on how well it meets each criterion and use the matrix to narrow down your options.

**Follow-up**: Reflect on how the decision matrix helped you refine your ideas. Did it help you identify the best solution?

|       | Ease | Impact | Cost | Total Score |
|-------|------|--------|------|-------------|
| Idea1 | 10   | 5      | 6    | **21**      |
| Idea2 | 8    | 8      | 8    | **24**      |
| Idea3 | 7    | 6      | 5    | **18**      |
| Idea4 | 9    | 6      | 7    | **22**      |
| Idea5 | 5    | 4      | 7    | **16**      |

*Fig. 5.4 Example of Decision Matrix (Scoring 10–Best, 1-Worst)*

## 3. Lateral Thinking with Random Word Association

**Objective**: Break free from conventional thinking patterns by making unexpected connections.

**Exercise**: Pick a random word and try to connect it to a problem you are working on. How can that word inspire new ideas or approaches to the problem?

**Follow-up**: Reflect on how lateral thinking helped you generate new ideas. Did any unexpected insights emerge?

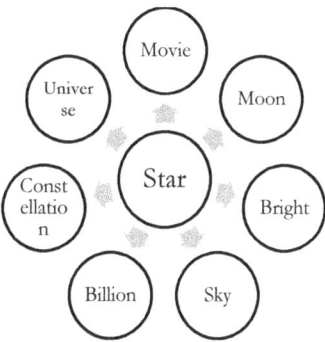

*Fig. 5.5: Example of Random Word Association*

## 4. Root Cause Analysis for Convergent Thinking

**Objective**: Use root cause analysis to drill down into the underlying cause of a problem.

**Exercise**: Take a current challenge and ask "why" five times to uncover the root cause. For example, if a project is behind schedule, keep asking why until you identify the core issue.

**Follow-up**: Reflect on how root cause analysis helped you identify the underlying problem. How can you address that problem more effectively?

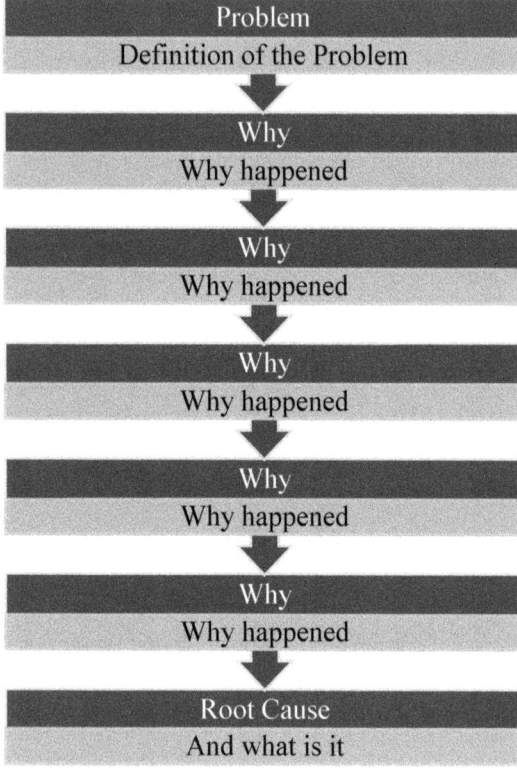

Fig. 5.6: Example of a 5-Why Analysis Template

## Conclusion: Cognition as the Engine of Creative Growth

In the alchemy of creative excellence, cognition plays the role of water—nourishing, shaping, and refining ideas. It allows creative excellence to flow freely through divergent thinking while also providing the structure needed to turn those ideas into practical solutions through convergent thinking.

By balancing these two cognitive processes—much like water moves between states—we can ensure that creative excellence does not remain abstract but leads to meaningful outcomes. Cognition is what allows us to take the raw sparks of curiosity and courage and turn them into fully formed, actionable solutions.

In the next chapter, we will explore how **collaboration**, the fertile soil, provides the environment in which creative excellence can flourish even more, amplifying the effects of cognition by bringing together diverse perspectives and skills.

## Chapter 6
# Collaboration: The Catalyst for Creative Alchemy

*"Coming together is a beginning, staying together is progress, and working together is success." Henry Ford*

In the alchemy of creative excellence, Collaboration is the catalyst that expedites the magic in the crucible of creative alchemy. While cognition shapes and refines ideas, it is through collaboration that this process accelerates, gaining energy and momentum. Just as a catalyst speeds up a chemical reaction without being consumed, collaboration enriches the creative process, bringing diverse perspectives, insights, and expertise into the mix. It ignites new possibilities, challenges assumptions, and sharpens ideas in ways that solitary effort cannot. In the alchemist's creative journey, collaboration transforms individual sparks of brilliance into a collective blaze of innovation, turning potential into reality at a much faster pace ion.

In the metaphor of Creative Excellence Garden, Collaboration is the fertile land where ideas take root and grow. Just as a plant requires fertile soil to fully develop, creative excellence flourishes when individuals come together, pooling their diverse perspectives, skills, and experiences. Without collaboration, even the most promising ideas might wither, lacking the collective nourishment needed to transform them into meaningful outcomes.

**Transactive Memory Systems (TMS)**, introduced by Daniel Wegner in the late 1980s and expanded by researchers like Wegner, Moreland, and Levine, underscores the value of diversity in skills and industry within collaborative teams. TMS highlights that teams with a broad range of expertise can effectively store, access, and utilize specialized knowledge, leading to enhanced innovation. When a team with diversity in skills and industry is coupled with proper coordination and structured communication, it can produce exceptional results. Each team member's unique expertise contributes to a collective knowledge base, enabling the team to approach complex problems creatively and efficiently. Structured communication ensures that team members are aware of each other's strengths and know how to leverage the necessary expertise at the right time, ultimately leading to innovative and impactful solutions.

> Creative Collaboration =
> 
> (Diversity × Coordination × Communication)

In the previous chapters, we explored how curiosity is the seed of creative excellence, how courage acts as sunlight to nurture and sustain ideas, and how cognition is the water that refines and directs those ideas. Now, we turn our attention to collaboration, the fertile land that allows creative excellence to thrive. In this metaphor, collaboration provides the environment in which ideas can grow stronger and more robust, benefiting from the synergy of multiple minds working together toward a shared goal.

Just as a plant grows best in rich, fertile soil where nutrients are abundant, creative excellence reaches its full potential in a collaborative environment that nurtures diverse contributions.

Collaboration is not just about working together; it is about creating a space where ideas can cross-pollinate, grow, and evolve into something greater than the sum of their parts. In this chapter, we will explore how collaboration amplifies creative excellence, the cognitive and emotional dynamics of teamwork, and practical strategies for cultivating effective collaboration.

## The Power of Collective Creative excellence

Collaboration is where creative excellence transcends individual effort and becomes truly transformative. When we work with others, we expose ourselves to different perspectives, knowledge, and skills that broaden our thinking. In a collaborative environment, creative excellence becomes more expansive as each participant brings their unique strengths and insights to the table.

Imagine a fertile field where various plants—each representing a different idea—are growing together. Some ideas are stronger in one area, while others bring different nutrients to the collective creative landscape. In this fertile environment, ideas can intermingle, cross-pollinate, and grow stronger together. The synergy created by collaboration allows us to achieve more than we ever could on our own.

In the context of creative alchemy, collaboration is essential for transforming individual sparks of curiosity, courage, and cognition into something larger and more impactful. It provides the foundation for complex, innovative solutions that require the input and expertise of multiple minds.

## Cognitive Benefits of Collaboration

Collaboration engages both **divergent** and **convergent thinking** on a larger scale, enriching the creative process. When individuals with diverse backgrounds and expertise come together, they bring unique perspectives that can push the boundaries of **divergent thinking**. This diversity of thought fosters a broader exploration of ideas, enabling the team to consider possibilities that might not have occurred to any single individual.

Convergent thinking also benefits from collaboration. While divergent thinking generates a wide range of possibilities, convergent thinking allows the group to collectively evaluate these ideas, apply critical thinking, and refine them into actionable solutions. The collaborative environment encourages constructive feedback, where team members challenge each other's assumptions, ask probing questions, and sharpen the ideas being developed.

This collaborative process is akin to cultivating a fertile field—different plants contribute unique qualities to the soil, enriching it for its growth. Likewise, collaboration enriches the creative process by integrating diverse viewpoints, leading to more well-rounded and innovative solutions.

The **Manhattan Project** during World War II is a striking example of group flow in action. This monumental effort brought together some of the greatest scientific minds of the 20th century—physicists, engineers, chemists, and military experts—to develop the first atomic bomb. The success of the project depended on the collaborative efforts of individuals with diverse expertise who worked together to solve complex technical challenges under immense pressure.

The Manhattan Project demonstrated the power of collaboration in both **divergent** and **convergent thinking**. Scientists had to explore radical new theories (divergent thinking) while simultaneously refining them into a practical, functional device (convergent thinking). The result was a breakthrough that changed the course of history—an outcome that could not have been achieved by any individual working in isolation.

## Group Flow: The Peak of Collaborative Creative excellence

Psychologist **Mihaly Csikszentmihalyi** introduced the concept of "flow," a mental state of deep focus and immersion in a task. When applied to collaboration, **group flow** occurs when a team works together in perfect harmony, producing creative outcomes that are greater than any individual contribution could achieve alone.

Group flow is like a well-cultivated field where every plant thrives in harmony with its environment, receiving the nutrients, sunlight, and water it needs to grow. In a state of group flow, team members feed off each other's energy and ideas, creating a seamless exchange of thoughts and a shared commitment to achieving a common goal.

When a team experiences group flow, creative excellence accelerates. Ideas are generated, evaluated, and refined more efficiently because everyone is working in sync, contributing their best efforts toward a shared vision. In this environment, creative excellence flourishes, much like plants in a fertile field where every element is perfectly balanced.

## Emotional Dynamics in Collaboration

While collaboration can be incredibly rewarding, it is also emotionally complex. Working with others requires **trust**, **openness**, and a willingness to navigate differences of opinion. Just as fertile soil must be carefully maintained to ensure the growth of healthy plants, collaborative environments require attention to emotional dynamics to foster positive interactions and successful teamwork.

One of the key emotional challenges in collaboration is managing **conflict**. When diverse perspectives come together, disagreements are inevitable. However, these conflicts can be productive, as they push teams to think critically and challenge assumptions. The key is to embrace healthy conflict and use it to explore new ideas and develop more robust solutions.

Trust is another essential ingredient in successful collaboration. For individuals to contribute their best ideas, they need to feel safe and supported by the group. **Amy Edmondson's theory of "psychological safety"** emphasizes the importance of creating an environment where team members feel comfortable sharing ideas without fear of judgment or retribution. When teams establish a foundation of trust and psychological safety, they create the conditions for open communication, creative excellence, and risk-taking.

Pixar's **Braintrust** is a prime example of how trust and collaboration can lead to extraordinary creative outcomes. Braintrust is a group of directors, writers, and animators who come together to give feedback on each other's work during the development of a film. These sessions are known for their candor—team members are encouraged to offer honest, constructive criticism without sugarcoating their feedback.

What makes Braintrust successful is the **culture of trust** that underpins it. Directors understand that the feedback they receive is intended to improve their films, not to undermine their authority or creative vision. This trust allows for open dialogue, where team members can challenge each other's ideas in a way that leads to better outcomes. The result is that Pixar consistently produces high-quality, innovative films that resonate with audiences worldwide.

## The Role of Diversity in Collaboration: Enriching the Creative Soil

One of the greatest benefits of collaboration is the diversity it brings to the creative process. Just as a field with a variety of plants creates a more resilient ecosystem, teams that are diverse in their backgrounds, experiences, and perspectives bring unique insights that enrich the creative process.

Diverse teams are more likely to generate innovative solutions because they approach problems from a variety of angles. Studies have shown that diverse teams outperform homogeneous ones, particularly in tasks that require creative excellence and problem-solving. The more perspectives a team can draw from, the more likely they are to discover new and innovative solutions.

Lin-Manuel Miranda's creation of the musical Hamilton is a powerful example of how diversity can enhance collaboration. Miranda brought together a diverse cast and crew to tell the story of America's founding fathers through the lens of hip-hop, R&B, and traditional musical theater. The creative fusion of these different styles, combined with the diverse backgrounds of the performers, resulted in a groundbreaking production that resonated with audiences in ways that traditional musicals had not.

The success of Hamilton demonstrates how diversity in collaboration can lead to innovative outcomes that push the boundaries of what is possible. By bringing together different cultural influences and perspectives, Miranda was able to create something entirely new and impactful.

# Collaboration in Non-Corporate Settings: Expanding the Creative Field

While many examples of collaboration come from the corporate world, the principles of collaboration apply equally well in non-corporate settings. In fact, some of the most transformative innovations have come from **scientific research**, where collaboration is essential for advancing knowledge.

### Example: The Human Genome Project:

The **Human Genome Project** was a collaborative effort involving scientists from multiple countries working together to map the entire human genome. This ambitious project required the expertise of geneticists, biologists, computer scientists, and mathematicians. The collaboration allowed researchers to pool their resources and knowledge, accelerating the pace of discovery and achieving a monumental scientific breakthrough that has since revolutionized medicine and biology.

The success of the Human Genome Project demonstrates how collaboration across disciplines can lead to groundbreaking discoveries that have a profound impact on society. In this case, collaboration was not just a convenience—it was a necessity. The scale of the project was so vast that no single individual or team could have completed it alone.

### Fostering Collaboration in Creative Alchemy

Just as a fertile field must be carefully tended to ensure that plants grow strong and healthy, collaboration requires intentional practices and strategies to thrive. Below are some practical exercises and tools to help build collaborative skills and foster a creative, productive environment.

## 1. Group Brainstorming Exercise

**Objective**: Encourage divergent thinking and generate creative ideas as a team.

**Exercise**: Gather your team and assign a problem or topic for brainstorming. Set a timer for 15 minutes and encourage everyone to contribute ideas freely. The key is to avoid judgment or evaluation during this phase—every idea, no matter how unconventional, should be considered. After the brainstorming session, shift to convergent thinking by evaluating the ideas together and selecting the most viable ones for further development.

**Follow-up**: Reflect on the group's dynamics during the brainstorming session. How did the diversity of perspectives enhance the creative process? Were there moments of conflict, and if so, how were they resolved?

## 2. Trust-Building Exercise: Share Vulnerabilities

**Objective**: Build trust and psychological safety within the team.

**Exercise**: Have each team member share a story about a time they took a creative risk that did not work out as planned. The goal is to normalize failure and create a space where team members feel comfortable sharing both successes and setbacks. This exercise helps build trust and empathy, which are essential for effective collaboration.

**Follow-up**: Reflect on how sharing vulnerabilities affected the group dynamic. Did it strengthen trust and openness? How might this exercise influence future collaboration?

## 3. Conflict Resolution Role-Play

**Objective**: Practice managing conflict constructively in a collaborative setting.

**Exercise**: Divide the team into pairs and assign each pair a scenario in which they must resolve a creative conflict (e.g., two team members disagreeing on the direction of a project). Have each pair role-play the conflict and practice resolving it in a constructive manner. Afterward, discuss the different strategies used and what worked well.

**Follow-up**: Reflect on the importance of healthy conflict in collaboration. How can your team apply these conflict resolution strategies in real-world situations?

## Crowdsourcing: The Power of Collaborative Innovation

Crowdsourcing is a collaborative approach that harnesses the collective intelligence of individuals to achieve significant outcomes. By engaging a diverse community in problem-solving, idea generation, and resource mobilization, crowdsourcing empowers participants to contribute their unique skills and perspectives. This dynamic form of collaboration has proven effective across various fields, demonstrating its capacity to drive innovation and creative excellence.

One prominent example of crowdsourcing is **LEGO Ideas**, a platform that allows fans to submit their designs for new LEGO sets. Users can share their creative concepts, and if a design garners enough votes from the community, it is considered for production by LEGO. This initiative not only taps into the interests of the customer base but also fosters a sense of ownership among fans, who feel directly involved in the product development process. Successful designs, such as the LEGO NASA Apollo Saturn V, showcase how collaboration with the community can lead to innovative and commercially viable products.

**Threadless** serves as a compelling illustration of crowdsourcing in the creative realm. This online apparel store invites artists and designers worldwide to submit their t-shirt designs, which are then voted on by the community. The most popular designs are produced and sold, with the artists receiving a share of the profits. This model fosters creative excellence and engages the community in the selection process, creating a platform where artists can gain recognition and contribute directly to the brand's offerings.

Lastly, **Foldit** represents an innovative approach to scientific discovery through crowdsourcing. This online puzzle video game engages players in folding proteins in three-dimensional space, leveraging their collective intelligence to solve complex biological problems. Players work collaboratively to find optimal configurations for protein structures, contributing to scientific research and advancements in medicine. This example illustrates how crowdsourcing can lead to breakthroughs in scientific inquiry through an engaging and participatory format.

In summary, crowdsourcing as a form of collaboration exemplifies the power of community engagement in driving innovation, creative excellence, and problem-solving. By leveraging diverse perspectives and skills, organizations and individuals can achieve outcomes that are more innovative and impactful than what any single contributor could accomplish alone. Whether in product development, navigation, creative arts, funding, or scientific research, the effectiveness of crowdsourcing continues to demonstrate the profound potential of collective effort.

## Overcoming Challenges in Collaboration

While collaboration offers many benefits, it also presents challenges that must be managed to ensure success. One common challenge is **group thinking**, which occurs when the desire for harmony or consensus within a group leads to poor decision-making. Groupthink can stifle creative excellence and prevent the team from exploring diverse perspectives.

To overcome group thinking, teams must actively encourage dissenting opinions and alternative viewpoints. Leaders can play a critical role in fostering a culture where disagreement is welcomed as a valuable part of the creative process. It is important to create an environment where team members feel comfortable voicing their concerns or proposing unconventional ideas without fear of judgment.

Another challenge is balancing **individual contributions** with **group cohesion**. While collaboration requires individuals to work together toward a common goal, it is essential to recognize and value the unique contributions of each team member. Teams that strike this balance are more likely to achieve their creative potential.

### Practical Tool: The Six Thinking Hats:

**Edward de Bono's Six Thinking Hats** is a collaborative tool that helps teams approach problems from different perspectives, ensuring that all angles are considered. Each "hat" represents a different mode of thinking:

1. **White Hat**: Focuses on facts and data.

2. **Red Hat**: Considers emotions and gut feelings.

3. **Black Hat**: Identifies potential risks and challenges.

4. **Yellow Hat**: Looks for benefits and positive outcomes.

5. **Green Hat**: Encourages creative excellence and new ideas.

6. **Blue Hat**: Manages the overall thinking process.

By assigning different hats to team members or rotating hats during discussions, teams can ensure that all perspectives are considered, helping to overcome groupthink and promote a more balanced and thorough approach to problem-solving.

## Collaboration as the Foundation for Creative Alchemy

As we move from the exploration of **cognition** in the previous chapter to the power of collaboration, it becomes clear that creative excellence is not a solitary endeavor. While cognition refines ideas and pushes us toward practical solutions, collaboration amplifies that process by bringing together diverse minds to tackle complex challenges.

In the metaphor of **creative alchemy**, collaboration is the fertile land that allows the seeds of curiosity, courage, and cognition to grow and thrive. It provides the nourishment and support needed for ideas to take root and develop into fully realized innovations.

Collaboration is the foundation upon which many of the greatest innovations are built. Whether in business, science, the arts, or education, the ability to work effectively with others is crucial for turning creative ideas into reality. The strength of collaboration lies in its ability to harness the collective intelligence of a group, producing outcomes that are more innovative, impactful, and enduring than what any individual could achieve alone.

In the next chapter, we will explore how **consistency**, the gardener of creative excellence, plays a vital role in sustaining creative excellence and innovation over the long term. Just as collaboration brings together diverse perspectives to spark creative breakthroughs, consistency ensures that those breakthroughs are nurtured and developed into lasting success.

# Chapter 7
# Consistency—The Oxygen that Sustains the Creative Flame

*"Success is the sum of small efforts, repeated day in and day out." Robert Collier*

In our journey through the Creative Alchemy process, we have explored how curiosity sparks creative excellence, how courage fuels it into flames, how the crucible of cognition facilitates the transformative process, and how collaboration acts as a catalyst to expedite it. Now, consistency emerges as the oxygen that keeps the creative flame alive. While curiosity ignites the initial idea and courage fuels its growth, it is consistency that sustains the process over time. Just as a flame needs a steady supply of oxygen to burn brightly, creative excellence requires ongoing effort and attention to thrive. Consistency ensures that momentum is maintained that ideas are continuously nurtured, and that progress is achieved, even in the face of obstacles. Without consistency, the creative flame would flicker and fade. It provides the discipline and persistence necessary to turn fleeting inspiration into lasting innovation.

In the flourishing Garden of Creative Excellence, curiosity plants the seed of innovation, courage shines as the sunlight nurturing these budding ideas, and cognition provides the water that fuels their growth. Consistency, the steadfast gardener, is the vital force that tends to this vibrant ecosystem, ensuring that seedlings of inspiration grow into strong, lasting results. Without consistency, even the fertile soil of collaboration and the nurturing power of cognition would not be enough to see the creative process through to full fruition.

Creative excellence is not a one-time event, nor is it simply a flash of inspiration followed by immediate success. Instead, it is a long-term endeavor that requires regular attention and care, much like a garden that must be watered, pruned, and maintained daily. Consistency is the driving force that ensures your creative efforts grow over time, multiplying their impact and turning scattered ideas into lasting innovations.

### The multiplication factor of creative excellence

In many ways, consistency acts as the **multiplication factor** in creative excellence. While curiosity, courage, and cognition are vital, they remain ineffective without the regular, sustained efforts that consistency brings. Just as the garden flourishes when it receives constant attention, creative excellence thrives when you consistently show up, even when the path ahead is unclear or progress feels slow.

*The Creative Alchemy*

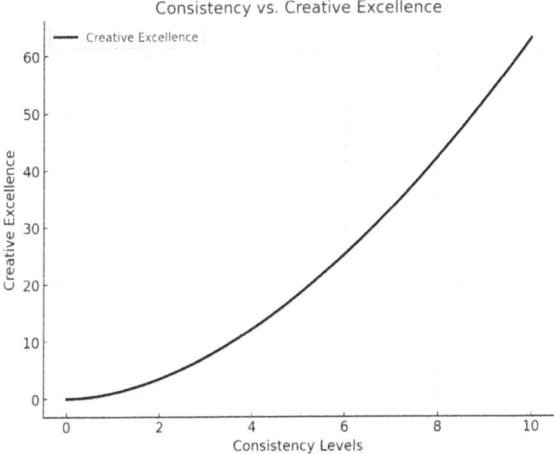

When we think about creative excellence, we often imagine it as a series of individual moments—flashes of inspiration or big breakthroughs. But, creative excellence works more like a compounding process. Each creative effort builds upon the last, gradually leading to greater and more significant outcomes. Like a gardener who plants seeds, waters them daily, and watches them grow, the effects of creative excellence compound over time when tended to consistently.

This idea of **multiplication rather than addition** is crucial in understanding how small, daily efforts add up to something much larger. If you write 500 words every day, by the end of the year, you will have written 180,000 words—several books' worth of content. Consistent effort does not just add up incrementally; it multiplies your capacity to achieve greater results.

Consider the act of practicing any creative skill, whether it's painting, music, writing, or even problem solving. Each day's practice builds on the previous day's work, and over time, you see exponential improvements. Like tending a garden where small, regular actions—like watering or weeding—lead to a healthy, flourishing landscape, your creative efforts grow stronger the more you nurture them through consistent practice.

## Consistency and the Power of Habit

The key to consistency lies in the formation of **habits**. Habits are the foundation for long-term creative success because they remove the need for constant motivation or willpower. Once a behavior becomes a habit, it becomes automatic—just like brushing your teeth or checking your email in the morning. You no longer must decide whether to do it; it is simply part of your routine.

In his book Atomic Habits, **James Clear** emphasizes the power of small, incremental changes in building long-term success. He argues that focusing on tiny improvements, repeated consistently, leads to remarkable transformations over time. In the context of creative excellence, this means that establishing small, daily habits can lead to exponential growth.

Clear's **four-step framework** for habit-building—cue, craving, response, and reward—can be easily applied to creative pursuits. For example, if you want to develop the habit of writing every morning, you can establish a cue by setting a specific time (such as right after breakfast), associate the writing session with something pleasurable (like your favorite cup of coffee), and reward yourself with a sense of accomplishment afterward. Over time, the consistency of this routine will make writing feel natural, almost automatic, just like a well-cared-for garden that grows steadily with daily attention.

## Consistency as a Process, Not an Event

Consistency transforms creative excellence from an occasional event into a sustainable process. Like growing a garden, creative excellence requires regular attention, even when there are no immediate signs of progress. While there will be moments of inspiration when everything seems to click, there will also be periods when progress feels slow or even stagnant. The key is to **trust the process** and keep showing up.

The creative process is full of **peaks and valleys**. There will be bursts of inspiration when ideas flow easily, but there will also be stretches where progress seems slow or blocked. Just as a gardener knows that plants grow even when you cannot see the roots beneath the soil, the same is true for creative excellence. Growth often happens beneath the surface, and the cumulative effect of showing up consistently leads to breakthroughs when you least expect them.

## Real-Life Example: J.K. Rowling's Persistence

Perhaps one of the most famous examples of creative consistency is **J.K. Rowling** and her journey to publish Harry Potter. Before becoming one of the most successful authors of all time, Rowling faced numerous rejections from publishers who did not believe in her story.

Struggling financially and facing personal hardships, she could have easily given up on her dream.

However, Rowling remained **consistent**. She kept writing, editing, and improving her manuscript, even in the face of countless setbacks. Eventually, her persistence paid off, and the Harry Potter series became a global phenomenon. Rowling's success is a testament to the power of consistency, not just talent. She did not achieve her dream in one moment of genius but through daily effort and an unwavering commitment to her craft.

## Consistency and Mastery

**Mastery**, much like gardening, is about nurturing something over the long term. In his book Mastery, **George Leonard** argues that achieving mastery in any skill requires commitment, patience, and consistent practice. Mastery is not a destination; it is a lifelong journey of continuous improvement, marked by both steady progress and inevitable plateaus.

Leonard describes mastery as a series of **small, incremental improvements** that accumulate over time. These small steps may seem insignificant on their own, but when practiced consistently, they lead to a significant progress. This approach applies to all creative fields, whether you are an artist, writer, engineer, or entrepreneur. The more consistent you are in practicing your craft, the closer you get to mastery.

Like a gardener who learns to tend their plants through trial and error, creative mastery comes from persistent practice. Each day of consistent work brings new insights, new skills, and new growth. Just as plants do not grow overnight, creative mastery is built through years of practice and patience.

## Building Confidence Through Consistency

Consistency is also closely linked to **confidence**. The more consistently you engage in a creative activity, the more confident you become in your abilities. Confidence does not come from a single moment of success but from the accumulation of small victories over time. As you develop a consistent creative practice, you build trust in yourself and your ability to push through obstacles.

For example, if you are a writer, showing up every day to write, regardless of how well the words flow, builds your confidence in your ability to produce. Over time, you begin to trust the process, recognizing that even on challenging days, you are still making progress. This confidence grows stronger the more you consistently practice, creating a positive feedback loop: the more consistent you are, the more confident you become, and the more confident you become, the easier it is to maintain consistency.

## Exercises to Build Creative Consistency

1. **The 30-Day Consistency Challenge to develop a habit of practicing daily creative excellence** Choose one creative activity (writing, painting, coding, etc.) and commit to doing it every day for 30 days. Set a specific time and duration for the practice (e.g., 30 minutes every morning) and stick to it, even when you do not feel inspired. Follow-up: At the end of the 30 days, reflect on the impact of consistent

practice. What progress have you made? How has the habit of consistency influenced your creative confidence and motivation?

2. **Creative Consistency Journal to track creative progress:** Start a journal where you document your creative efforts each day. Write about what you worked on, the challenges you faced and how you overcame them. At the end of each week, review your entries and note any patterns or insights. Follow-up: After a month, reflect on how your consistent efforts have contributed to your creative progress. What small wins have you achieved, and how has your confidence grown because of consistent practice?

3. **Consistency in Collaboration to foster group efforts**

   If you are working on a collaborative project, set regular meetings with your team to review progress and ensure everyone is staying on track. Hold each other accountable for showing up consistently and contributing. Follow-up: Reflect on how the regular check-ins and consistent efforts have improved the team's overall progress. How has consistency within the group contributed to the success of the project?

## Conclusion: Consistency as the Key to Creative Success

In the world of creative excellence, **consistency is the gardener** that ensures your ideas grow and thrive. It multiplies the impact of curiosity, courage, and cognition, ensuring that each effort builds upon the last. Without consistency, even the most brilliant ideas would wither and fade. But with consistent practice, creative excellence becomes a powerful, sustainable force that leads to innovation and success.

As we move into the next chapter on overcoming conceptual blocks, remember that consistency is the foundation upon which all creative breakthroughs are built. Whether you are facing a mental roadblock, struggling with self-doubt, or feeling stuck in a creative rut, it is consistency that will see you through to the other side.

In the end, creative excellence is not a sprint but a marathon. It is not about the one-time burst of inspiration but about the daily practice of showing up, doing the work, and trusting that each small effort will lead to something greater. Consistency, more than any other factor, is what transforms creative ideas into lasting success.

## Chapter 8
## Purging Contaminants – Overcoming Conceptual Blocks

*"Conceptual blocks are like invisible walls in our thinking, limiting our ability to see new possibilities."*
– James L. Adams

In the journey toward creative excellence, we have explored how curiosity, courage, cognition, and consistency are integral parts of cultivating creative excellence. However, even with the right ingredients in place, we all encounter obstacles that can stifle creative excellence—what James L. Adams refers to as conceptual blocks. These mental barriers hinder our ability to think outside the box, and much like weeds in a fertile garden, they restrict growth unless it is identified and removed.

Conceptual blocks are the contaminants in the crucible of creative alchemy that can disrupt the delicate chemical reactions of innovation. These blocks have the potential to damage the transformative process, stifling ideas before they can fully form. Just like impurities in a chemical reaction, they need to be purged out to allow creative excellence to flow freely and for true breakthroughs to emerge

Imagine a garden filled with rich, fertile soil—each creative idea is like a seed ready to sprout and grow. But if left unattended, weeds will inevitably creep in, strangling the young plants and robbing them of nutrients. Conceptual blocks function in much the same way. Just as weeds compete for space, water, and sunlight, these mental barriers choke our ability to nurture creative thoughts, limiting their full potential. If we do not actively tend to our mental garden by identifying and removing these blocks, they can hinder the flourishing of our creative excellence.

Conceptual blocks can take many forms: cognitive biases, assumptions, past habits, or environmental factors that limit our thinking. The good news is that much like removing weeds, these blocks can be dismantled with the right strategies and mindset. By clearing these obstacles, we create room for our creative excellence to thrive, allowing us to unlock our full potential.

In this chapter, we will dive into the nature of conceptual blocks, explore the types that commonly impede creative excellence, and learn practical strategies to overcome them. By recognizing and working through these mental barriers, you will be better equipped to maintain the creative flow and open yourself up to new possibilities.

## What Are Conceptual Blocks?

Conceptual blocks are mental barriers that restrict creative thinking and problem-solving. These blocks limit our ability to perceive problems from new angles, generate novel ideas, or take creative risks. They are often deeply ingrained in our thinking processes and arise from cognitive biases, past experiences, or even societal norms.

James L. Adams, in his seminal work Conceptual Blockbusting, identified four primary types of conceptual blocks that hinder creative excellence:

1. **Constancy**: The tendency to rely on familiar methods and patterns of thinking.
2. **Commitment**: Over-attachment to past ideas, assumptions, or methods, even when they no longer serve us.
3. **Compression**: narrowing the problem too early, thus limiting exploration of alternative solutions.
4. **Complacency**: Growing comfortable with current thinking, assuming that further innovation is unnecessary.

| Type | Description | Example |
|---|---|---|
| Constancy | Tendency to stick to one perspective | Focusing solely on past solutions |
| Commitment | Over-commitment to a point of view | Ignoring new possibilities because of previous experiences |
| Compression | Narrow focus on problems | Missing important |

|  |  | information or details |
|---|---|---|
| Complacency | Lack of curiosity and engagement | Avoiding asking questions or exploring alternatives |

Each of these blocks serves as a mental barrier, restricting creative thinking. In the same way that weeds can choke a garden's growth, conceptual blocks prevent ideas from flourishing. Let us explore these blocks in detail, understand their implications, and examine how we can break through them to achieve creative flow.

## Constancy: The Trap of Sticking to Fixed Patterns

Constancy is the conceptual block that occurs when we become fixated on a single way of thinking. This block manifests in our tendency to rely on familiar methods or processes when solving problems rather than exploring alternative approaches.

A common example of constancy is functional fixedness, a cognitive bias that limits our ability to see new uses for familiar objects. In the famous Candle Problem experiment, participants were asked to attach a candle to a wall in such a way that it would not drip wax onto the table. Given only a candle, a box of tacks, and matches, most people struggled because they viewed the box as merely a container for the tacks, not as a potential platform to hold the candle. Their constancy in perceived the box in a fixed way limited their ability to solve the problem.

**Example: Kodak's Decline** A powerful real-world example of constancy is Kodak's failure to embrace digital photography. Despite having invented one of the first digital cameras, Kodak's reliance on its traditional film-based business model blinded the company to the potential of digital technology. This attachment to its past success resulted in Kodak losing its dominance in the photography market.

**Overcoming Constancy: Lateral Thinking** To break free from the rigidity of constancy, we can use lateral thinking, a technique popularized by Edward de Bono. Lateral thinking involves approaching problems from unexpected angles rather than following a linear path. This method encourages us to challenge assumptions and explore unconventional solutions.

## Exercise: Challenging Assumptions

- Objective: Break free from habitual thinking by questioning core assumptions.

- Exercise: Identify a problem you are currently facing. Write down all your assumptions about the problem (e.g., "This method always works," "We need more resources to solve this"). Then, systematically challenge each assumption. What if the opposite were true? What if this assumption were not a constraint?

- Reflection: How did challenging these assumptions open new possibilities? What creative solutions emerged when you moved beyond fixed thinking patterns?

## Commitment: The Risk of Over-Attachment to Ideas

Commitment refers to our attachment to familiar ideas, methods, or strategies, even when they are no longer effective. This block prevents us from exploring new options because we are emotionally or mentally committed to past solutions that once worked but are now limiting.

Overcommitment to a single idea or process is dangerous because it blinds us to alternative approaches. We often become stuck in patterns of thinking that have been successful in the past, even when innovation requires us to let go of these old patterns.

**Example: Microsoft's Zune** Microsoft's Zune, a competitor to Apple's iPod, is an example of commitment leading to failure. Instead of rethinking its approach to portable music players, Microsoft committed to creating a product like the iPod rather than innovating in new ways. As a result, the Zune failed to capture significant market share, and the product line was eventually discontinued.

**Overcoming Commitment: The "Kill Your Darlings" Strategy** A powerful way to break free from overcommitment is to apply the "kill your darlings" strategy, a concept often used in writing. This approach encourages us to let go of our favorite ideas, no matter how attached we are to them, if they are no longer serving the larger goal.

## Exercise: The "Kill Your Darlings" Review

- Objective: Develop the ability to detach from ideas that no longer serve your project.

- Exercise: Review a current project you are working on. Identify the elements you are most attached to—your "darling" ideas. Then ask yourself, "If I had to remove one of these elements, which would it be, and why?" Letting go of a beloved idea might open space for more innovative solutions.

- Reflection: Did removing a "darling" idea create opportunities for more effective or creative approaches? How did this exercise impact your overall project?

## Compression: Narrowing the Problem Too Early

Compression occurs when we define a problem too narrowly, prematurely limiting our exploration of potential solutions. This block often arises when we feel pressured to solve a problem quickly, which can prevent us from considering a wide range of creative alternatives.

When we compress our thinking, we focus on specific details or constraints, missing the bigger picture. In doing so, we restrict the potential for innovation because we fail to explore the full scope of the problem.

**Example: The Wright Brothers** Wright Brothers avoided the compression trap by taking a broad approach to problem-solving. Instead of focusing solely on propulsion, they explored multiple aspects of flight—such as control, balance, and lift. Their holistic view allowed them to develop the first successful powered aircraft.

**Overcoming Compression: Divergent Thinking To combat compression, we can turn to divergent thinking, which encourages us to expand the range of possibilities before narrowing them down. This process helps us explore creative solutions that may initially seem unrelated or impractical.**

**Exercise: The "10x Brainstorm"**

- **Objective:** Expand your thinking by pushing beyond obvious solutions.

- **Exercise:** Take a problem you are working on and challenge yourself to brainstorm 10 times more ideas than you typically would. For example, if you usually generate 5 ideas, push for 50. The goal is to generate quantity, not quality—do not worry about whether the ideas are practical.

- **Reflection:** Review your expanded list of ideas. Were there unexpected connections or solutions that emerged from this broader exploration?

## Complacency: The Danger of Comfort Zones

Complacency is the mental block that arises when we stop challenging ourselves to think creatively because we have grown comfortable with routine or past successes. This block prevents further innovation by encouraging us to rest on our laurels instead of continuing to push boundaries.

**Example: Blockbuster's Downfall** Blockbuster's failure to adapt to the rise of Netflix is a prime example of complacency. While Netflix embraced the future of media streaming, Blockbuster remained committed to its traditional rental model, assuming its success would continue. By failing to innovate, Blockbuster was eventually overtaken and went out of business.

**Overcoming Complacency: The Growth Mindset** Overcoming complacency requires us to embrace a growth mindset, a concept developed by psychologist Carol Dweck. A growth mindset is the belief that skills and abilities can be developed through dedication and effort. This mindset encourages continuous learning and improvement, pushing us beyond our comfort zones.

## Exercise: The Continuous Improvement Challenge

- **Objective:** cultivate a habit of continuous growth and innovation.

- **Exercise:** Identify an area of your life or work where you have grown complacent. Set a goal to learn something new or improve your skills in this area over the next month. For example, take a course, read a book, or seek feedback from a mentor.

- **Reflection:** At the end of the month, reflect on what you have learned. How has this challenge pushed you out of your comfort zone? What new possibilities has it opened?

## Techniques for breaking conceptual blocks

Now that we have explored the four main types of conceptual blocks, let's dive into some practical techniques for breaking them down:

## The Alchemical Process of Overcoming Conceptual Blocks

To transform these conceptual blocks into steppingstones for creative excellence, we can adopt various strategies, much like an alchemist employs different techniques to purify materials. Here are some effective methods:

- **Make the Strange Familiar and the Familiar Strange**: By using analogies and metaphors, we can connect unfamiliar problems to those we understand well. This not only helps in defining the problem more clearly but also allows us to see it from a fresh perspective. For instance, consider the exploration of space travel. If we view the complexities of interstellar travel as akin to navigating a vast ocean, we can brainstorm ways to overcome challenges by drawing parallels with maritime exploration—considering the importance of navigation, resource management, and crew dynamics.

- **Elaborate on Definitions**: Challenge yourself to generate multiple definitions for a single problem. This can be facilitated through a question checklist that prompts exploration of different angles. For example, if you are exploring the concept of creative excellence itself, ask, "What does creative excellence mean in different fields, such as art, science, and business?" or "What are the various barriers to creative excellence?" This expansive thinking can reveal new dimensions and insights.

- **Reverse the Problem Definition**: Thinking in opposites can lead to unexpected insights. If the challenge is to foster collaboration in a team, consider what might happen if collaboration were discouraged. Such a reversal forces us to reconsider our assumptions and may lead to innovative solutions, like finding ways to improve communication that might not have been obvious at first.

- **Defer Judgment**: In brainstorming sessions, it's crucial to focus on quantity over quality. The wildest ideas often spark the most creative solutions. By suspending judgment, we create a safe space for all ideas to flourish before evaluating their feasibility. For example, when exploring new product ideas, encourage team members to suggest any concept, no matter how unconventional, to foster an environment ripe for creative exploration.

- **Expand Current Alternatives**: Use subdivision to break problems into smaller components. This technique encourages a broader exploration of potential solutions. For example, when examining the design of a new product, consider various components like aesthetics, functionality, user experience, and environmental impact. By dissecting the product into these elements, new alternatives may surface.

- **Combine Unrelated Attributes**: Integrate seemingly unrelated ideas to generate new alternatives. Techniques such as morphological synthesis encourage us to blend different attributes, thereby uncovering innovative applications. For instance, consider the convergence of technology and health. Merging concepts from wearable technology with fitness training can lead to innovative applications like smart clothing that monitors physical activity and vital signs in real time.

- **Janusian Technique**: This approach encourages considering contradictory ideas simultaneously. Named after the Roman god Janus, who looked in opposite directions, it helps reconcile seemingly opposing ideas to find innovative solutions. For example, when developing a marketing strategy, think about how to attract customers while also considering how to discourage others. This duality can help identify unique selling propositions and target demographics more effectively.

- **Reverse Brainstorming**: This technique challenges assumptions by considering the opposite of what you are trying to achieve. For example, instead of brainstorming how to improve a process, brainstorm ways to make it worse. This reverse perspective can help identify potential pitfalls or overlooked opportunities. If you were to plan an event, considering ways to ensure it fails could illuminate critical factors that need to be addressed for success.

## Conclusion: Moving Beyond Conceptual Blocks

Conceptual blocks are inevitable in the creative process, but they do not have to be permanent barriers. By understanding the nature of these blocks—whether it is the rigidity of constancy, the overcommitment to past ideas, the narrowing of compression, or the comfort of complacency—we can begin to break them down.

The strategies and exercises outlined in this chapter are designed to help you move past these mental barriers and unlock your full creative potential. Whether it is using lateral thinking to break free from fixed patterns or adopting a growth mindset to push past complacency, the key is to remain flexible, open, and willing to challenge your own assumptions.

## Chapter 9
# Creative excellence in Action: Real-World Case Studies

Creative excellence is not just an abstract concept—it's the powerful force that drives groundbreaking innovation across industries and fields. From transforming businesses to advancing healthcare, the elements of the **Creative Excellence Equation—curiosity, courage, cognition, collaboration, and consistency**—come together to foster revolutionary breakthroughs. This chapter explores real-world case studies that highlight how these components blend to tackle challenges, solve complex problems, and achieve success. These examples span both corporate and non-corporate settings, illustrating the versatility and effectiveness of the Creative Excellence Equation.

Each case study demonstrates how creative principles have been applied in different fields, showcasing the dynamic use of curiosity to explore, courage to take risks, cognition to structure ideas, collaboration to multiply efforts, and consistency to sustain progress. As you read through these examples, consider how the same principles can be applied to your own work and life.

## Case Study 1: Tesla's Electric Vehicles: Courage and Consistency

Tesla has reshaped the automotive industry, leading the charge in the development of electric vehicles (EVs). Founder **Elon Musk's** vision for a sustainable energy future and his courage to disrupt an entrenched market paved the way for Tesla's success. At a time when the industry was dominated by gasoline-powered cars, Musk's willingness to challenge this paradigm showed immense courage. Despite widespread skepticism, Tesla forged ahead with electric vehicle technology.

Tesla's journey also exemplifies the power of consistency. It did not just launch an electric car and stop there. Instead, the company continuously improved battery technology, introduced cutting-edge autonomous driving features, and worked tirelessly to reduce production costs. These consistent efforts have allowed Tesla to remain at the forefront of the EV market, making electric vehicles more accessible to the mass market.

## Key Elements of the Creative Excellence Equation:

- **Courage**: Musk's boldness in challenging the dominant gasoline-powered car market.

- **Consistency**: Tesla's relentless commitment to improving battery efficiency, production processes, and vehicle design over time.

## Case Study 2: Apple's iPhone: Curiosity and Cognition

When Apple introduced the iPhone in 2007, it completely revolutionized the mobile phone industry. The driving force behind this innovation was **Steve Jobs'** curiosity—he questioned why mobile phones couldn't offer a more seamless, intuitive user experience. By thinking beyond the limitations of physical keyboards, Jobs and his team developed the groundbreaking touchscreen interface that changed the way users interact with their devices.

The success of the iPhone was not just about curiosity; it also required cognition. Apple's engineering and design teams employed divergent thinking to brainstorm multiple innovative solutions and then used convergent thinking to refine the best ideas into a practical, sleek device. This systematic approach allowed Apple to transform a bold idea into a product that set new standards for user experience and revolutionized the smartphone market.

## Key Elements of the Creative Excellence Equation:

- **Curiosity**: Steve Jobs' exploration of how to break away from traditional mobile phone designs.

- **Cognitive**: Apple's structured approach to refining the iPhone's design and user interface through iterative prototyping and problem-solving.

## Case Study 3: Netflix's Transition to Streaming: Commitment and Adaptation

Netflix started as a DVD rental service but transformed itself into one of the world's most dominant streaming platforms. This dramatic shift was driven by the company's commitment to staying ahead of technological trends and its ability to adapt to changing consumer demands. Recognizing the potential of online streaming, Netflix made the bold decision to shift away from its successful DVD rental model, even though streaming technology was still in its infancy at the time.

Netflix's ability to adapt did not stop there. The company moved into producing original content, such as House of Cards and Stranger Things, further cementing its position as a leader in the entertainment industry. Netflix's commitment to investing in modern technologies and its flexibility in adapting its business model have kept it at the forefront of the industry, showcasing how innovation thrives when companies are willing to pivot in response to new opportunities.

## Key Elements of the Creative Excellence Equation:

- **Commitment**: Netflix's long-term investment in new technologies and trends.

- **Adaptation**: Its flexibility in transitioning from a DVD rental model to a streaming platform and original content creation.

## Case Study 4: IDEO's Design Thinking: Collaboration and Cognition

IDEO is a global design and innovation firm known for pioneering the concept of design thinking, a human-centered approach to problem-solving. IDEO's success stems from its emphasis on collaboration—its teams are composed of diverse designers, engineers, and strategists who work together to generate creative solutions. This interdisciplinary approach allows for the integration of multiple perspectives, leading to more innovative and user-centered products.

IDEO also excels at balancing cognition. The firm uses divergent thinking to brainstorm a wide array of possibilities and convergent thinking to narrow those ideas down into viable, practical solutions. By encouraging interdisciplinary collaboration and structured cognitive processes, IDEO has helped create groundbreaking products across various industries, from healthcare to consumer goods.

### Key Elements of the Creative Excellence Equation:

- **Collaboration**: IDEO's interdisciplinary teamwork that generates diverse perspectives and innovative ideas.
- **Cognition**: The structured thinking process that refines creative ideas into actionable solutions.

## Case Study 5: COVID-19 Vaccine Development: Curiosity, Collaboration, and Commitment

The rapid development of COVID-19 vaccines is one of the most significant scientific achievements in modern history. Faced with a global health crisis, pharmaceutical companies displayed intense curiosity by exploring novel approaches like mRNA technology to develop effective vaccines in record time.

Collaboration was crucial in overcoming the logistical and scientific hurdles of vaccine development. Government agencies, pharmaceutical firms, and research institutions worked together across borders to ensure swift development, testing, and distribution of vaccines. Additionally, the scientific community's commitment to overcoming obstacles under immense pressure led to the rapid development of vaccines, saving millions of lives worldwide.

**Key Elements of the Creative Excellence Equation:**

- **Curiosity**: The exploration of novel technologies, like mRNA, to tackle the COVID-19 pandemic.

- **Collaboration**: unprecedented cooperation between governments, researchers, and pharmaceutical companies.

- **Commitment**: The dedication to ensuring rapid, safe vaccine development and distribution under immense pressure.

## Case Study 6: Pixar's Storytelling: Curiosity and Collaboration

Pixar has become synonymous with innovation in the field of animated films. At the heart of Pixar's success is its constant curiosity—the studio continually seeks new ways to push the boundaries of animation and storytelling. For example, Toy Story broke new ground as the first full-length computer-animated film, but Pixar did not stop there. The studio continues to explore new techniques, from photorealistic rendering in Finding Nemo to emotionally rich narratives in Inside Out.

Pixar's storytelling process is highly collaborative, involving teams of writers, animators, and technical experts. This collaboration enables the studio to create richly layered films that resonate with audiences on both technical and emotional levels. By encouraging curiosity and collaboration, Pixar has maintained its position as a leader in both technology and storytelling.

**Key Elements of the Creative Excellence Equation:**

- **Curiosity**: Pixar's drive to constantly explore new storytelling techniques and animation technology.
- **Collaboration**: The teamwork between animators, writers, and technical experts that elevates Pixar's films.

**Case Study 7: Jane Goodall's Groundbreaking Work with Chimpanzees: Curiosity, Courage, and Consistency**

Jane Goodall's pioneering research on chimpanzees revolutionized the field of primatology and changed our understanding of human evolution. Goodall's curiosity about animal behavior drove her to enter the African wilderness at a time when few women pursued fieldwork in science. She had no formal academic training in primatology but was determined to learn through direct observation.

Goodall's courage is evident in her decision to live alone in Gombe National Park, working in challenging conditions and facing dangers from the wild animals she studied. At the time, her methods of close interaction with chimpanzees were unconventional, but she persisted despite skepticism from the scientific community. Her findings, such as the discovery that chimpanzees use tools, were groundbreaking and reshaped the way we think about primates.

Goodall's consistency over decades of field research is another key to her success. Despite facing personal and professional challenges, she returned to Gombe year after year, building an unmatched body of knowledge about chimpanzees. Her long-term commitment to conservation and education continues to inspire new generations of scientists and activists.

## Key Elements of the Creative Excellence Equation:

- **Curiosity**: Goodall's relentless exploration of animal behavior and her desire to understand chimpanzees.
- **Courage**: Her willingness to break societal norms and work alone in the wild.
- **Consistency**: Her lifelong dedication to studying and conserving chimpanzees.

## Case Study 8: The Apollo 13 Mission: Collaboration and Cognition

The Apollo 13 mission in 1970 is a legendary example of how collaboration and cognition can solve life-or-death problems. When an oxygen tank exploded during the mission, it left the spacecraft severely damaged and its crew in danger of not returning to Earth. NASA engineers and astronauts faced a massive challenge: they had to work with the limited resources available on the damaged spacecraft to solve problems like oxygen supply, carbon dioxide levels, and energy consumption.

The collaboration between the astronauts onboard Apollo 13 and the ground control team at NASA was critical to the crew's survival. Engineers had to use creative problem-solving (cognition) to repurpose available materials and find solutions to challenges that had never been encountered before. The famous phrase "failure is not an option" became the driving force behind this remarkable collaborative effort, which resulted in all three astronauts returning safely to Earth.

## Key Elements of the Creative Excellence Equation:

- **Collaboration**: The teamwork between NASA engineers and astronauts to solve complex problems in real time.

- **Cognition**: creative thinking and problem-solving under intense pressure, using available resources in novel ways.

## Case Study 9: Community Farming Projects in Urban Areas: Curiosity, Collaboration, and Commitment

In many urban areas, community farming projects have transformed abandoned lots into green spaces that provide fresh food, educate residents, and foster community. These projects begin with curiosity—residents questioning how to address food insecurity and improve their environment. By exploring the potential of urban spaces, community members develop creative solutions to local problems.

## Case Study 10: SpaceX and the Mars Mission

Elon Musk, a visionary known for his exceptional creative excellence, has led SpaceX to revolutionize space travel. His ambition to colonize Mars is a remarkable demonstration of the Creative Excellence Equation, where each dimension plays a critical role in pushing the boundaries of what was once deemed impossible.

1. **Curiosity:** Musk's curiosity about space travel, paired with his extensive technical knowledge, became the cornerstone for SpaceX's most groundbreaking innovation: reusable rockets. In an industry where single-use rockets were the norm, Musk questioned why space travel could not be made more affordable and sustainable. His intellectual curiosity about long-distance space exploration led to the idea of reusing rockets, an approach that most industry experts had never seriously entertained. This relentless curiosity about how space travel could evolve—coupled with his deep understanding of

physics, engineering, and business—propelled SpaceX toward developing technologies that could dramatically reduce the cost of space missions.

2. **Courage**: One of the defining traits of Musk's leadership at SpaceX has been his extraordinary courage in the face of repeated setbacks. In its early years, SpaceX faced multiple rocket failures, each one threatening to bankrupt the company. These failures were not just technical issues; they represented massive financial losses that put Musk's entire vision at risk. However, Musk's ability to take risks, even when it meant risking personal fortune and the future of his company, showed incredible courage. His willingness to continue after catastrophic failures like the Falcon 1 rocket's first three unsuccessful launches is a powerful example of how courage drives creative excellence. Musk's belief in the goal of making space travel more accessible and colonizing Mars pushed him to persevere through adversity, a key factor in SpaceX's eventual success.

3. **Cognition**: At the core of SpaceX's success is the company's data-driven approach to problem-solving—an essential component of cognition within the Creative Excellence Equation. Every failure, such as the early Falcon rocket crashes, became an opportunity for learning and improvement. SpaceX's engineers used detailed analysis of data from each failed launch to inform design improvements for future iterations. This iterative process of cognitive refinement allowed them to steadily improve their

rocket designs, leading to more successful launches. The concept of reusable rockets also stemmed from Musk's ability to apply first principles thinking—a cognitive approach where complex problems are broken down into their most basic elements. By questioning assumptions and stripping down problems to their core, SpaceX was able to tackle challenges in ways that traditional aerospace companies had not.

4. **Overcoming Conceptual Blocks**: The aerospace industry had long accepted that space travel required massive budgets and that rockets were a one-time use technology. This concept of expendable rockets became a significant mental block for the entire industry. SpaceX, however, broke through this conceptual block by developing rockets that could be recovered and reused, dramatically lowering the costs associated with space exploration. Overcoming this deeply entrenched belief required not only cognitive agility but also the courage to challenge industry norms. By thinking outside the box and questioning established paradigms, SpaceX fundamentally shifted how the world approaches space travel, making the previously unthinkable a reality.

5. **Collaboration**: SpaceX's success was not built on individual genius alone—it was a collective effort. Collaboration across diverse fields was crucial in solving the technical, logistical, and scientific challenges of space travel. Musk, though a visionary leader, recognized the importance of surrounding himself with the best engineers, scientists, and

technicians from around the globe. From developing the advanced materials needed for rockets to perfecting the landing systems, SpaceX's collaborative environment fostered innovation. Teams from various disciplines—software development, mechanical engineering, aerospace science—worked together, combining their expertise to create groundbreaking technology like the Falcon Heavy and the Starship rockets. This multidisciplinary collaboration exemplifies how large-scale, innovative projects require not just individual brilliance but also the collective creative excellence of diverse teams working in unison.

6. **Consistency**: Finally, SpaceX's relentless pursuit of innovation through consistent testing and improvement has been fundamental to its success. SpaceX does not just aim for occasional breakthroughs; the company is built on a culture of continuous iteration and testing. Whether it's refining rocket engines or improving landing precision, SpaceX conducts countless tests, each one building on the lessons of the latest. The company's ability to make consistent progress, even after setbacks, is a testament to the role of persistence in creative excellence. Through this consistency, SpaceX was able to achieve one of its most significant milestones—the successful landing and reuse of the Falcon 9 rocket in 2015, which marked a turning point for the space industry. This steady progress toward reusable space technology has not only enabled cost-

effective missions but also laid the groundwork for SpaceX's larger goal: the colonization of Mars.

In conclusion, SpaceX's journey to revolutionize space travel and its ambitious mission to colonize Mars is a masterclass in the application of the Creative Excellence Equation. Elon Musk and his team leveraged curiosity to explore new possibilities, had the courage to face and learn from failures, used cognitive processes to refine their innovations, broke through conceptual blocks that constrained the industry, fostered collaboration across various disciplines, and remained consistent in their pursuit of success. This case study shows how blending these dimensions can lead to transformative innovations that reshape entire industries.

The success of these urban farming initiatives also depends on collaboration. Volunteers, local governments, and environmental organizations come together to pool resources and knowledge. Community members work collectively to plant, maintain, and harvest crops while collaborating with local schools and businesses to promote sustainability.

Consistency plays a critical role in the long-term success of these projects. Community members must remain committed to maintaining the gardens, organizing workshops, and educating new participants. Through their combined efforts, these urban farming projects not only improve food security but also strengthen community bonds.

## Key Elements of the Creative Excellence Equation:

- **Curiosity**: Community members questioning how to address urban food insecurity.

- **Collaboration**: Residents, volunteers, and organizations working together to create sustainable farming projects.

- **Commitment**: The ongoing efforts to maintain and expand the gardens for future generations.

## The Creative Excellence Equation in Action— Putting It All Together

Now that we have explored the components of the Creative Excellence Equation, it is clear that these elements are not just individual skills—they work together to amplify creative potential across different fields. Whether you are in the arts, business, science, or technology, the Creative Excellence Equation provides a structured way to approach innovation and problem-solving. Each of the case studies discussed shows how combining **curiosity, courage, cognition, collaboration,** and **consistency** leads to groundbreaking solutions and lasting success.

As you move forward in your own creative endeavors, consider how to apply these principles holistically. Use curiosity to ask bold questions, summon courage to take risks, employ cognition to refine your ideas, collaborate with others to leverage diverse perspectives, and maintain consistency to see your ideas come to fruition. Just like the visionaries and innovators in these examples, you can unlock creative breakthroughs by embracing the full power of the Creative Excellence Equation.

## Steve Jobs: Melding Cognition and Collaboration for Innovation

Steve Jobs is an iconic figure who perfectly embodied the Creative Excellence Equation. His deep curiosity about design, technology, and user experience led him to question traditional product development. Jobs demonstrated courage in pursuing risky innovations, like the iPhone, which fundamentally changed the mobile industry. His cognitive abilities allowed him to distill complex technologies into simple, elegant designs, ensuring that Apple's products were not just innovative but also user-friendly. Jobs worked collaboratively with teams of engineers and designers, and his ability to foster collaboration across disciplines was key to Apple's success. His consistency in maintaining a long-term vision for design and technological excellence allowed Apple to become a leader in the tech industry. Jobs also overcame conceptual blocks that limited others by believing in a future where technology would be seamlessly integrated into everyday life.

**Marie Curie: Pioneering Scientific Discovery with Curiosity and Courage:** Marie Curie's boundless curiosity drove her to explore the mysteries of the natural world, particularly in the realm of radioactivity. Despite the challenges she faced as a woman in a male-dominated field, Curie's courage allowed her to push forward with her research, even when it posed physical risks. Her cognitive abilities enabled her to conduct meticulous experiments and apply scientific reasoning to make groundbreaking discoveries, such as isolating radium and polonium. Collaboration was also a key to her success—working alongside her husband Pierre Curie and later her daughter Irène, she fostered partnerships that furthered her research. Curie's consistency in pursuing her work, even after personal tragedies, led her to receive two nobel prizes in two different fields. She overcame conceptual blocks by questioning established scientific beliefs, forever changing the way scientists understood radioactivity and atomic structure.

## Zaha Hadid: Redefining Architecture with Cognitive and Collaborative Excellence

Architect Zaha Hadid revolutionized the field of architecture by continually pushing the boundaries of what was possible. Her curiosity about form, space, and fluidity in design allowed her to break free from the rigid structures of traditional architecture. Hadid's courage in defying conventional norms, despite early rejection, paved the way for her visionary ideas to be realized. She had an exceptional cognitive ability to bring abstract designs to life through technical precision, balancing artistic freedom with structural logic. Hadid's work was also highly collaborative, requiring her to engage with engineers, material scientists, and construction experts to turn her avant-garde designs into functional buildings. Her consistency over decades of work allowed her to become one of the most celebrated architects of her time, overcoming conceptual blocks by challenging the notion that buildings must conform to rigid, geometric forms.

## Dr. Stephen Seiler: Innovating Sports Science Through Curiosity and Collaboration

In the world of sports science, Dr. Stephen Seiler's curiosity led him to challenge traditional endurance training models. His questioning of the existing methods led to his groundbreaking research on polarized training, a concept that has since transformed how elite athletes' train. Seiler demonstrated courage by presenting his findings despite skepticism from the sports science community. His cognitive approach involved meticulous data collection and analysis, which enabled him to refine his theories and present a model that was both simple and effective. Seiler's collaborative efforts with coaches, athletes, and other scientists helped bring his research into practical application, ultimately benefiting elite athletes across various sports. His consistency in pursuing long-term research ensured that his ideas gained traction over time. By overcoming the conceptual block that moderate-intensity training was superior, Seiler unlocked a new understanding of how athletes could maximize performance through better training practices.

These visionaries illustrate how leveraging the dimensions of the Creative Excellence Equation—curiosity, courage, cognition, collaboration, and consistency—can lead to revolutionary breakthroughs. Whether in technology, science, architecture, or sports, their ability to overcome conceptual blocks and persist through challenges enabled them to push the boundaries of their respective fields and leave a legacy.

## Reflective Exercise: Applying the Creative Excellence Equation to Your Own Life

1. **Curiosity + Knowledge**: What are you most curious about? What areas of knowledge can you deepen to fuel your creative pursuits?

2. **Courage**: Think about a time when fear or doubt held you back from pursuing a creative idea. How can you develop the courage to move past those fears in the future?

3. **Cognition**: When you generate ideas, how do you structure and refine them? Can you improve your ability to balance divergent and convergent thinking?

4. **Conceptual Blocks**: What conceptual blocks are holding you back right now? How can you challenge or break through those barriers?

5. **Collaboration**: Who can you collaborate with to enhance your creative excellence? What strengths do others bring to the table that can complement your own?

6. **Consistency**: How can you ensure consistency in your creative efforts? What small, daily actions can you take to build momentum over time?

## Conclusion: The Equation for Lasting Creative excellence

The Creative Excellence Equation is not merely a tool for sparking ideas; it is a comprehensive framework for sustaining innovation and transforming creative thoughts into tangible, impactful solutions. Each component—curiosity, courage, cognition, collaboration, and consistency—serves a critical role in ensuring that creative excellence is not fleeting but evolves and grows over time.

Throughout this book, several examples from diverse fields have demonstrated how individuals and organizations leveraged these dimensions of the Creative Excellence Equation to achieve groundbreaking results. Whether it is Elon Musk's revolution of space travel, Steve Jobs' reshaping of consumer technology, or Marie Curie's pioneering work in science, these stories illustrate how powerful this holistic approach can be in overcoming challenges and fostering lasting innovation.

As you prepare to move into the final chapter, which will bring together all the elements discussed so far, it's essential to recognize that the Creative Excellence Equation is an ongoing, dynamic process. Obstacles are inevitable, but overcoming conceptual blocks is part of the creative journey. With curiosity to explore new possibilities, courage to take risks, cognitive skills to analyze and refine ideas, collaboration to broaden perspectives, and consistency to see your efforts through, the path to creative excellence is always within reach.

Remember, creative excellence is not a destination but a continuous journey of growth and exploration. The Creative Excellence Equation is your guide to navigating this journey, helping you turn challenges into opportunities and ideas into reality.

## Chapter 10
# Conclusion: Mastering the Creative Excellence Equation

As we conclude our exploration of creative excellence, it is clear that creative excellence is not a rare gift but a skill anyone can cultivate. The **Creative Excellence Equation**—curiosity, courage, cognition, collaboration, and consistency—offers a roadmap for turning ideas into reality. This Equation is not just about fleeting moments of inspiration, but about creating a sustained force that drives innovation and meaningful change.

Each element in the Equation plays a unique role. **Curiosity, courage, cognition, and collaboration** are the **additive elements**. These elements build upon each other to fuel the creative process. **Curiosity** sparks new ideas, **courage** pushes you to take risks, and **cognition** refines those ideas into structured solutions. **Collaboration** then enhances creative excellence by bringing diverse perspectives together, enriching the process and building on the contributions of others.

**Consistency** is the **multiplicative element** that amplifies the impact of the additive factors. It ensures that the creative process is sustained over time, multiplying the effects of curiosity, courage, cognition, and collaboration by maintaining momentum and focus. Consistency keeps the creative process alive and thriving, ensuring long-term growth and progress.

On the other hand, **conceptual blocks** act as the **divisive element**, hindering creative excellence by stifling ideas, creating doubt, or slowing down progress. These blocks, like contaminants in the alchemy process or weeds in a garden, can divide and weaken the flow of creative excellence. Removing these obstacles is essential for creative excellence to flourish.

Throughout the book, we have explored these ideas through two metaphors: **creative alchemy** and the **creative garden**. In alchemy, creative excellence transforms raw ideas into something valuable, while in the garden metaphor, creative excellence grows like a plant, needing nurturing and care. Both metaphors emphasize how the elements work together to ensure creative success.

In conclusion, creative excellence requires balance, care, and persistence. The **Creative Excellence Equation** offers the tools to navigate this journey. With curiosity, courage, cognition, and collaboration as the additive elements, consistency as the multiplier, and awareness of conceptual blocks as divisive forces to address, you can turn fleeting inspiration into lasting innovation.

| Garden Metaphor | Alchemy Metaphor | Creative Excellence |
|---|---|---|
| **Curiosity** | | |
| The seed that plants creative excellence | The spark that ignites the creative process | Sparks new ideas & drives exploration |
| **Courage** | | |
| The sunlight that gives energy to creative excellence | The fuel that turns sparks into flames | Empowers you to take risk and explore new thoughts |
| **Cognition** | | |
| The water that nurtures and refines ideas | The crucible where raw ideas are shaped | Divergent & Convergent thinking to shape creative ideas |
| **Collaboration** | | |
| The fertile soil that helps ideas grow and multiply | The catalyst that accelerates the creative process | Diverse perspectives for greater innovation. |

| Consistency | | |
|---|---|---|
| The gardener that tends and ensures growth | The oxygen that sustains the creative flame. | Compounding effect through sustained practice |
| **Conceptual Blocks** | | |
| Weeds that can damage the garden | Contaminants that threaten the process. | Mental barriers that restrict creative thinking |

## Practical Steps to Embody the Creative Excellence Equation

### 1. Stay Curious:

- Regularly explore new perspectives and topics outside your comfort zone.
- Challenge the status quo by asking, "What if?" and "Why not?" each day.
- Make time to explore the unknown, feeding your creative mind with fresh insights.

### 2. Act with Courage:

- Take calculated risks, stepping beyond your comfort zone.
- Embrace failure as an inevitable part of the creative journey. Every setback is an opportunity for growth.

- Push through fear and uncertainty, knowing that true innovation lies beyond the familiar.

3. **Sharpen Your Cognition:**
   - Use creative tools like brainstorming, mind mapping, and lateral thinking to generate ideas.
   - Employ structured approaches like SWOT analysis or decision matrices to refine those ideas.
   - Balance divergent (creative) thinking with convergent (analytical) thinking to develop well-rounded solutions.

4. **Collaborate and Build Networks:**
   - Engage with people from diverse fields to challenge your assumptions.
   - Foster an environment of open dialogue and shared learning within your teams.
   - Seek regular feedback to refine and elevate your ideas through collaboration.

5. **Cultivate Consistency:**
   - Dedicate time each week to creative work, even if it is in small increments. Creative excellence is a practice.
   - Break large projects into smaller tasks, celebrating each step forward.
   - Maintain long-term focus, understanding that the creative process often takes time to bear fruit.

## Overcoming conceptual blocks with the Creative Excellence Equation

The journey toward creative excellence is not without its obstacles; conceptual blocks, much like **weeds in a garden**, threaten to hinder progress. These blocks, whether they stem from fear, rigid thinking, or limited resources, can stop creative excellence in its tracks. But with the **Creative Excellence Equation**, these blocks can be overcome.

- **Use Curiosity to Uproot Weeds:** Reframe challenges by asking different questions or exploring alternative perspectives. New viewpoints often reveal solutions hidden by mental blocks.

- **Harness Collaboration to Break Free:** Bring fresh voices into the conversation. Often, a new perspective from a different discipline can unlock the solution to a long-standing problem.

- **Stay Consistent:** Progress may be slow, but pushing through conceptual blocks requires patience and persistence. Creative excellence often requires sustained effort before breakthroughs emerge.

## The Creative Excellence Equation in Action: Putting It All Together

The **Creative Excellence Equation** works across industries and disciplines, helping people achieve lasting innovation. Visionaries like **Steve Jobs**, **Marie Curie**, **Elon Musk**, and **Zaha Hadid** have applied these principles to reshape industries, spark scientific revolutions, and elevate human achievement. But this Equation is not exclusive to them—it is available to you.

These leaders embraced **curiosity** to ask new questions, relied on **courage** to break through barriers, used **cognition** to solve complex problems, fostered **collaboration** to enhance their creative impact, and practiced **consistency** to ensure long-term success. By confronting and overcoming conceptual blocks, they were able to unlock the full potential of their creative visions.

The Creative Excellence Equation gives you the same power to navigate challenges, expand your creative potential, and turn vision into reality.

## A Call to Action: Unleash Your Creative Excellence

**Now is your moment to act.** The Creative Excellence Equation is more than a concept—it is a guide, a strategy, and most importantly, a call to action. You now possess the tools, the insights, and the roadmap. The next step is yours to take.

The world is in dire need of fresh ideas, bold solutions, and innovative ways of thinking. Whether it is tackling societal challenges, advancing technology, or solving personal or professional problems, **the power to create real change is within you**. Creative excellence is not just something to admire from afar; it's an active force that can transform your life, your work, and the world around you.

**Do not wait for the perfect moment—create it.** Start today. Plant the seeds of curiosity, water them with cognition, shine the light of courage on them, collaborate to fertilize the soil, and nurture your ideas with the gardener of consistency.

Be the catalyst for creative excellence in your field. Use **curiosity** to question, **courage** to act, **cognition** to refine, **collaboration** to amplify, and **consistency** to persevere. These are the essential ingredients for unlocking creative excellence, and they are all within your reach.

The **Creative Excellence Equation** is your guide for a lifetime of innovation. Apply it relentlessly—today, tomorrow, and every day thereafter. **Transform challenges into opportunities, ideas into innovations, and dreams into reality.**

**The journey begins now. Will you take the next step and unleash your creative excellence?**

# References

1. Adams, J. L. (2001). *Conceptual blockbusting: A guide to better ideas*. Perseus Publishing.
   - Introduces conceptual blocks and strategies to overcome them, essential for enhancing creative thinking and problem-solving.

2. Brown, T. (2009). *Change by design: How design thinking creates new alternatives for business and society*. Harper Business.
   - Explores how design thinking can drive innovation and solve complex problems across industries.

3. Bono, E. (1992). *Lateral thinking: Creativity step by step*. Harper & Row.
   - de Bono's work on lateral thinking is relevant to the cognition component of the Creative Excellence Equation, particularly how divergent and convergent thinking contribute to creative problem-solving.

4. Dweck, C. S. (2006). *Mindset: The new psychology of success*. Ballantine Books.

- Examines how a growth mindset fosters creative excellence and success by embracing challenges and learning from failure.

5. Eberle, B. (1971). *SCAMPER: Games for imagination development*. Prufrock Press.
   - A framework for expanding ideas and encouraging creative thinking through structured games and exercises.

6. Gordon, W. J. J. (1961). *Synectics: The development of creative capacity*. Harper & Brothers.
   - Describes the Synectics method, which emphasizes making unfamiliar things familiar and familiar things strange to foster creativity.

7. IDEO. (Various Publications).
   - IDEO's human-centered design and innovation principles are explored in their various publications, exemplifying practical applications of design thinking.

8. Kelley, T., & Kelley, D. (2013). *Creative confidence: Unleashing the creative potential within us all*. Crown Business.
   - Offers inspiration and strategies for unlocking creativity, emphasizing confidence in one's creative abilities.

9. Kolb, D. A. (1984). *Experiential learning: Experience as the source of learning and development*. Prentice Hall.

- Explores how hands-on experience fosters creativity and personal development through Kolb's learning cycle.

10. Medawar, P. (1967). *The art of the soluble*. Methuen.
    - Discusses how problem solving in science is driven by framing problems in a way that makes them solvable.

11. Osborn, A. F. (1953). *Applied imagination: Principles and procedures of creative problem-solving*. Scribner.
    - Outlines brainstorming techniques and group problem-solving methods to stimulate creativity.

12. Ries, E. (2011). *The lean startup: How today's entrepreneurs use continuous innovation to create radically successful businesses*. Crown Publishing Group.
    - Introduces the principles of iterative development, minimum viable products (MVPs), and continuous innovation in business.

13. Rothenberg, A. (1979). *The Emerging Goddess: The Creative Process in Art, Science and Other Fields*. University of Chicago Press.
    - Introduces Janusian thinking, the ability to hold two contradictory ideas at once, as a method for fostering creativity.

14. Sinek, S. (2009). *Start with why: How great leaders inspire everyone to act*. Portfolio.

- Discusses the role of purpose-driven leadership in inspiring creative excellence and innovation.

15. Sternberg, R. J. (1999). *Handbook of Creativity*. Cambridge University Press.
    - A collection of essays on creativity, covering cognitive processes, problem-solving techniques, and innovation research.

16. Von Oech, R. (1986). *A whack on the side of the head: How you can be more creative*. Warner Books.
    - Offers unconventional techniques and exercises for stimulating creativity and breaking through mental barriers.

17. Whetten, D. A., & Cameron, K. S. (2016). *Developing management skills* (9th ed.). Pearson.
    - A resource that provides tools and techniques for improving management and problem-solving skills, with a focus on creativity in leadership.

18. Isaacson, W. (2011). *Steve Jobs*. Simon & Schuster.
    - This biography gives insights into Steve Jobs' creative processes, especially related to Apple and the iPhone development, aligning with the section on cognition and courage.

19. Thomke, S. (2020). *Experimentation works: The surprising power of business experiments*. Harvard Business Review Press.
    - This reference is useful in discussing Netflix's willingness to experiment with streaming and

original content, a perfect example of courage and cognition in practice.

**20.** Amabile, T. M. (1996). *Creativity in context: Update to the social psychology of creativity*. Westview Press.
- Addresses environmental factors and how collaboration can enhance or inhibit creative excellence—relevant for the collaboration section (e.g., Pixar, IDEO).

**21.** Christensen, C. M. (1997). *The innovator's dilemma: When modern technologies cause great firms to fail*. Harvard Business School Press.
- Discusses how companies can struggle to adapt and how innovation often requires risk and adaptability, referencing companies like Netflix and Tesla.

**22.** Sutton, R. I. (2001). *Weird ideas that work: How to build a creative company*. Free Press.
- Sutton's insights on fostering creative excellence in organizations complement discussions on breaking cultural and perceptual blocks, particularly in tech companies like IDEO and Tesla.

**23.** Altidor, W. (2017). *Creative courage: Leveraging imagination, collaboration, and innovation to create success beyond your wildest dreams*. Wiley.
- Altidor explores how courage fuels creative excellence across industries, providing practical

guidance for applying creative courage in both personal and organizational growth.

**24.** Wallas, G. (1926). *The art of thought.* Harcourt, Brace and Company.
- Wallas' four stages of the creative process (preparation, incubation, illumination, and verification) highlight how creative excellence is a structured process, not a spontaneous occurrence.

**25.** Csikszentmihalyi, M. (1996). *Creativity: Flow and the psychology of discovery and invention.* HarperCollins.
- Csikszentmihalyi's research on flow provides insight into how creativity thrives when there is a balance between challenge and skill, supporting the structured nature of creativity.

**26.** Holiday, R. (2014). *The obstacle is the way: The timeless art of turning trials into triumph.* Portfolio.
- Focuses on how overcoming challenges leads to growth, relevant for sections on courage and creative excellence.

**27.** Duckworth, A. (2016). *Grit: The power of passion and perseverance*. Scribner.
- Explores the role of grit in success, particularly relevant to the courage section.

**28.** Maxwell, J. C. (2000). *Failing forward: Turning mistakes into steppingstones for success*. Thomas Nelson.
- Provides insights on how failure contributes to learning and creativity.

**29.** Waitzkin, J. (2007). *The art of learning: An inner journey to optimal performance*. Free Press.
- Discusses how learning and creativity are connected, especially useful for the cognition section.

**30.** Syed, M. (2015). *Black box thinking: Why most people never learn from their mistakes—but some do*. Penguin.
- Highlights the importance of learning from failure, which is crucial for innovation and creative excellence.

www.ingramcontent.com/pod-product-compliance
Lightning Source LLC
LaVergne TN
LVHW061615070526
838199LV00078B/7289